SECOND THOUGHTS

SELECTED PAPERS ON PSYCHO-ANALYSIS

.S., L.R.C.P.

WILLIAM HEINEMANN MEDICAL BOOKS LIMITED
LONDON

FIRST PUBLISHED 1967

© W. R. BION 1967

THIS VOLUME APPEARS UNDER THE
AUSPICES OF THE MELANIE KLEIN TRUST

Made in Great Britain at the Pitman Press, Bath

Contents

1 Introduction

It is customary to find in a book of collected papers on psycho-analysis, a number of case histories; this book is no exception. Ostensibly there is an account of the patient's history, some detailed reports of sessions with the patient's associations and the interpretations the analyst has given. It has always seemed to me that such reports are open to the objection that the narrative and the interpretations given are only two different ways of saying the same thing or two different things said about the same fact. With the years my suspicion has ripened into conviction. I have attempted to formulate this conviction in three books, Learning from Experience, Elements of Psycho-Analysis, and Transformations, each one carrying the discussion a little further and making the formulations more precise. Now the time has come to reprint old papers I find that the change in my views about psycho-analytic method makes me unwilling to let them go out without showing what that change is. For those who want the papers as they were originally printed, here the papers are, but I have added a commentary which involves an evolutionary change of opinion. I do not regard any narrative purporting to be a report of fact, either of what the patient said or of what I said, as worth consideration as a "factual account" of what happened. In the first place, I do not attribute to memory the significance it is usually given. The fact of involuntary distortions is so well established by psycho-analysis itself that it is absurd to behave as if our reports were somehow exempted from our own findings. Memory is born of, and only suited to, sensuous experience. As pyscho-analysis is concerned with experience that is not sensuous—who supposes that anxiety has shape, colour or smell?—records based on perception of that which is sensible are records only of the psycho-analytically irrelevant. Therefore in any account of a session, no matter how soon it may be made after the event or by what master, memory should not be treated as more than a pictorialized communication of an emotional experience. The accounts of cases in this book, though sincerely supposed by me at the time to be factually correct (I exclude alterations made and acknowledged on account of discretion), should now be regarded as verbal formulations of sensory images constructed to communicate in one form what is probably communicated in another; for example, as pyscho-analytic theory, either in the same paper or in some part of psycho-analytic literature. If this seems a harsh reassessment, I reply that progress in psycho-analytic work will cease unless this reassessment is seen to be essential; it should be the jumping off point for a new attitude to scientific work—others no less than our own. The papers are reprinted in their original form for those who find it easier to regard them as factual reports. I have added commentary to express my changed view.

2 The Imaginary Twin[1]

1. The patient from whose analysis I draw most of my material had had many years of psycho-therapy which ended when the therapist advised leucotomy. In view of a shocking family history and the strains to which the patient had been subjected in early childhood the doctor who referred him thought the outlook bad.

2. The patient had a sister 18 months' older than himself who died of a disease, from which both suffered, when the patient was one year old; both had severe diarrhoea during the course of the illness.

3. The family associated closely with their neighbours whose children, two girls, one two years' younger than my patient, the other seven years' younger, were his only playmates until he was ten. The younger died in an asylum before the war; the other still survives but in a state of incurable insanity, supposedly schizophrenia.

4. Disunited parents complicated his childhood. This was spent abroad in a country which was developing its football and other sports so that when it was discovered that he was an athlete, and intelligent, then the way seemed clear for a popular and successful career. But the family fortunes deteriorated and the domestic relationships with them, until at thirteen the boy had had a breakdown from which he made no adequate recovery though he returned to, and has continued in, work. His Mother died after years of chronic and painful illness, when he was 17; the Father, many years later. His circumstances were further complicated at the time of his Mother's death by the need to leave his native land and start afresh here.

5. When he came to me I saw a man of 43, just under 6 ft. in height, of wiry build, sallow complexion and dull expressionless features: by profession a teacher. The discussion of

[1] Read to the British Psycho-Analytical Society, 1 November, 1950.

his difficulties was perfunctory, carried on for his part in monosyllabic listlessness. He agreed without enthusiasm to give analysis a trial.

6. My account of the next two years must necessarily be compressed. The central theme of the analysis was contamination: he had to protect his head from the pillow by resting his head on his hand; he could not shake hands; he felt that he contaminated the bath on which he relied to give him a feeling of cleanliness and that it contaminated him back again.

7. He feared that he drank too much; he wondered if his penis was erect; he could not bear to have someone sitting behind him on a bus; it was equally contaminating if he sat behind someone.

He began to wonder if he felt sexual with his students; before long suspicion turned to certainty, and this made him feel unclean.

In his associations a big part was played by phantasied therapeutic injections which he had given, only to fear that his needle might not have been properly sterilized.

8. During the whole of the first two years, I had great difficulty in being able to determine, from his reactions, what validity to assign to my interpretations. I did, on two widely separated occasions, hear, from an extra-analytic source, that the patient was said to be greatly improved. I, myself, saw no improvement; nor was I able to remark, what I now believe to be true, that a change began to manifest itself in him at the end of this period. Till that time his intonation had been uniformly drained of emotion and his statements correspondingly difficult to interpret for they almost always had the ambiguous character which admitted of different meanings if one considered them now with one emotional content, now with another.

9. There was plenty of oedipal material, produced on a most superficial level, which I duly interpreted, to meet with a perfunctory response or none at all.

My awareness of a change in the analysis developed over a period of some three months. At first it seemed as if my interpretations were only meeting with more than usually stubborn indifference, and then as if I was a parent who was issuing ineffectual exhortations and warnings to a refractory child. In due course I pointed this out to him and a change, not easily formulated, occurred. There was still the dreary monotone of associations but there was now a quality which derived from what I can best describe as the rhythm of his associations. It was as if two quite separate co-existent scansions of his material were possible. One imparted an overpowering sense of boredom and depression; the other, dependent on the fact that he introduced regularly spaced pauses in the stream of his associations, an almost jocular effect as if he were saying "Go on; it's your turn".

10. Examining the matter still further, I noticed that the associations were all stale associations inviting a stale response. If I broke the rhythm, he showed signs of anxiety or irritability; if I continued to give the interpretations, which it now became clear he both invited and expected, there emerged a sense of having reached a dead-end. I was not surprised when he said to me in the early part of the next session, that he felt the treatment was getting nowhere and was doing no good: did I think, he very reasonably asked, that it was worthwhile going on?

11. I replied that though estimations of progress in analysis were difficult to make there was no reason why we should not accept his evaluation as correct. But, I added, before we pass on to consider what should be done about it, we need to know what is meant by treatment. It might mean psycho-analysis; in which case it would appear that some other method of approach to his problems would have to be sought. A perhaps more obvious meaning would be, psycho-analysis as practised by myself, in which case the remedy would lie in a change of analyst rather than a change of method. There was, however, yet another possibility. We had already had reason to suppose that alleviation of symptoms was sometimes achieved by factors incidental to analysis; for example, the sense of security obtained from feeling there was someone to go to. It was possible that he was unconsciously referring to some factor of that kind.

12. There was a silence and since we have now reached the

point at which I must introduce the topic to be discussed, I shall take this opportunity to place before you some details of the analysis of the previous years, which are necessary for an understanding of what follows.

These details were not at the time important, but belonged rather to the periphery of the main stream of his associations. They derived from the point at which he introduced some new episode or anecdote that he was recounting. Thus he would say about some story that it had been told him by his homosexual brother-in-law. Or else that it was while visiting such and such a friend that he experienced particularly distressing symptoms. His circle of acquaintances was very great and as the theme of the analysis derived from the content of the story, I had no reason to pay much attention to the various characters thus casually mentioned. It is to this aspect of his associations, now become central and not peripheral, that I must retrospectively turn.

13. But first I would draw your attention to this: he would say, "I was thinking of talking to Mr. X and telling him that etc., etc." One day my attention was arrested by some peculiarity of phraseology, or maybe it was the somewhat improbable character of the remark, and I asked if he meant he had actually said whatever it was he told me. "Oh, no," he replied, "I am just imagining it!" It then turned out that many conversations introduced by the phrase "I was thinking of talking to Mr. X" or "Mrs. Y" were imaginary conversations although not by any means all of them. I had mentioned then that it sounded as if no clear distinction was being made between the real and the imaginary, but at the time this feature had not the importance that it was now about to assume.

Among the characters to whom he had spoken, whether in fancy or fact, a considerable part was played by a man of his profession, of similar age, with the same symptoms as himself, married and with a family. He resided still on the Continent, worked full hours and with such success that no one even suspected he had any illness. This man was able to travel freely which my patient could not. My patient would seem to contrast himself unfavourably with him.

There was, as I have said, the homosexual brother-in-law, a man of the same age, perhaps stouter, but definitely homosexual and with an incestuous attraction, perhaps even relationship, with my patient's wife.

There was a man with whom my patient played tennis; of this character I heard no more than that he played tennis.

There were a number of students of his, psychological cases he would remark, that had sent him other students. There was even one who had sent him a psychological case and he had wondered if he had realized that he was a psychological case when he sent him. (The ambiguity in the use of the relative pronoun is not a failure in grammar but rather a masterly expression of the patient's ability to convey much information, too much information, concisely).

There was an unpleasant colleague, whom he had known as a child and who had been contemporaneous with him in school, and now taught close by, who occasionally looked after his students, but he was so unscrupulously thrusting that my patient proposed not to use him again.

14. Let us now return to the patient whom we left silent after my summary of the issues confronting him before he could make a decision about treatment: I asked him what he was thinking about.

He replied that he was thinking about a woman with rheumatic pain. "She's always complaining about something or other and I thought," he said, "that she's very neurotic. I just advised her to buy some amytal and packed her off."

This, I said, was probably a compact description of the treatment he was having from me, treatment of which he doubted the efficacy. My interpretations were felt by him to be vague complaints to which he paid scant attention; his associations were many of them stale associations employed more for the soporific effect they shared with amytal than for their informative value and designed to keep me employed without bothering him. But, I added, we should also consider how this situation was rendered tolerable for himself and I drew his attention to peculiarities in his behaviour, notably the rhythm of "association—interpretation—association" that indicated that I was a twin of himself who supported him in a jocular evasion of my complaints and thus softened his resentment. He could identify himself with any one of the three roles.

His response was striking. His voice changed and he said, in a depressed tone, that he felt tired and unclean. It was as if, in a moment, I had in front of me, unchanged in every respect the patient as I had seen him at the first interview. The change was so sudden as to be disconcerting. What on earth, I wondered, had happened to the twin and the complaining parent? It was as if he had swallowed them and was suffering the consequences.

That was the end of the session. When I had recovered from my surprise, I remembered that we had often had reason to suppose that he felt he had a poisonous family inside him but that was the first occasion on which I had had quite such a dramatic exhibition of himself in the act of introjecting objects.

15. At the next session, the patient reported that he had had a terrifying dream. It was this: he was driving in a car and was about to overtake another. He drew level with it and then instead of passing it kept carefully abreast of it. The rival car slowed down and stopped, he himself conforming to its movements. The two cars were thus parked side by side. Thereupon the other driver, a man much the same build as himself, got out, walked round to his door and leaned heavily against it. He was unable to escape as, by parking his car near to the other, he had blocked egress from the far door, while the figure blocked egress from his door. The figure leered menacingly at him through the window. He woke in terror, to remain filled with anxiety throughout the waking day.

16. I interpreted the dream thus: the menacing figure was myself who was also the imaginary twin of which he had last spoken at the previous session. The twin was imaginary because my patient had prevented the birth of the twin—there was in fact no twin. His use of a twin as a means of alleviating anxiety was therefore illegitimate and the twin was determined that he, the patient, should not now be born, or to put it in other words, achieve freedom or independence. He was thus shut in, both by the twin and by his own act in

parking his car so near the twin's car. The analysis had been the car from which I had not been allowed to emerge as a real being; the dream showed his fear that in the previous session I had become alive only to block his escape from analysis by using me as a personification of the bad part of himself from which he wished to be dissociated.

17. There now followed a period in which the prominent features of the analysis were exhibitions of introjection and projection, splitting, and, not least, personification of the split-off portions of his personality. In a sense there was nothing new about all this, but as at the same time his analysis became far more integrated and his fear of his mechanisms less pronounced, we were the more able to see them clearly for what they were. In retrospect, I could see how much the anxiety produced by interpretations, made before the emergence of the twin, derived not only from the content of his associations but from the mere fact that I was drawing attention to his intra-physic processes.

18. One result of the increased integration of his analysis was that I was able to see that certain of his associations announced the theme around which the work, probably of several sessions, would centre. I shall take advantage of this fact to confine the discussion to two associations only, leaving the reader to assume that the material on which I based my interpretations was infinitely more copious than this necessarily compressed account would suggest.

19. The first association was produced before a week-end when he was going away to stay with friends. Week-end holidays and even annual holidays had not been thought of as possible until some six months previously when he had taken his first holiday for many years, but they had now become fairly regular occurrences. He said, "I am leaving a locum in charge of my students: he is not very experienced —the same age as myself but I don't feel sure he will be able to cope. There is a girl who may become ill and she may have to be admitted to hospital. That would be fairly straightforward except that you have to know the ropes a bit or you may not get the child into hospital. Usually I have an arrangement with a doctor I know well by which he helps when I am away, but this has been mucked up by a misunderstanding."

From the subsequent working through of this, it emerged that I had been the person who had messed up the understanding between the two doctors by my interpretation of the twin and the consequent forcing back into himself of the twin. The locum was a split-off portion of himself lacking in some essential qualities and in particular the ability to introduce the girl into hospital. I suggested that the part of himself that he left in charge of the girl was a genitally impotent part.

20. After the week-end he told me that the locum had made a mess of things and had frightened one of his parents. My patient felt you had to be very careful what you said to parents and the locum had made her anxious by talking too openly about her child's illnesses. The result was that she wanted him in future and not the other man. He felt it was hardly worth employing a locum because you only had to do the work yourself anyway. In reply to a question of mine he agreed that even before the week-end he had worried about the locum. So, in a sense, the employment of the locum had not relieved him of any anxiety or responsibility. He objected that the parent made a lot of demands on him and half implied that she was sexually attracted to him.

I interpreted that I was the parent who complained about being left in charge of the inexperienced locum. As a result of his leaving me in charge of his inexperienced self I, in turn, had been able to say things which had very much upset him. His anxiety was that if he came to me as an experienced man, that is to say potent, then I made demands on him, particularly sexual demands, which he felt unable to meet.

21. He shifted uneasily on the couch and became tense; after a moment he replied, "I feel curled up and I am afraid that if I stay like this I shall have cramp. If I stretch out I shall become rigid and touch the pillow and contaminate it and get contaminated back again. I feel as if I were in the womb".

I said that the uterus here represented the limitations he felt he imposed upon himself by being compelled to come as the locum. We had throughout his analysis seen that he feared that with him violence and aggression took the place of sexuality. The fear of his aggression, closely linked in his mind with faeces, caused him to retreat to a position in which he felt constrained and confined and thus secure from the hatred that a less cramped position would release. In fact all that happened was that he resented more than ever a relationship which imposed these limitations on him. We might take it that his association indicated that he had retreated into the womb and feared being born; but it was necessary to consider what this meant in present terms; I suggested that it meant that he could not rely on the use to which he would put his capacity if he permitted himself to develop by reuniting the various splits in his personality—particularly in allowing hatred to return as a part of himself in his relationship with me. Nor did he feel sure of my response to this. He feared that if he were to have a relationship with me, both of us being experienced, it would be bound to issue in mutual hatred.

22. The session ended: and that night he had a dream with which he started the next session. I will only give a portion of it. He said that a man had presented him with a bill and then left the house. The bill was far too large. He followed to expostulate but the man rapidly disappeared, disregarding my patient's attempts to arrest his attention by tapping him on the shoulder. My patient felt overwhelmed with rage such as he had never felt before and awoke in terror. I reminded him of the previous session and his fear of what would happen if he left his cramped curled up position—this was the split-off hatred of myself and the demands, financial and otherwise, that I and the analysis made upon him.

He went on to speak of a psychiatrist whom he had met that day. The man had during the war been on a Board which my patient attended for re-categorization on psychiatric grounds but he had not recognized my patient. My patient had questioned him and elicited that he treated patients and considered some 50 sessions enough. My patient formed a very poor opinion of him and decided that he could never have done anything for my patient's troubles had he tried to cure them in 50 sessions. During this overtly friendly questioning he had felt an intense hatred of him. My patient added that he still felt tense. I said that he was comparing me favourably with the psychiatrist, but the incident was produced as a warning of the interrogation to which I would be subjected were our roles reversed.

23. By this time, his relationship with me had become altogether more realistic and he showed every sign of co-operating in the investigation of his problem. It was possible, as it had never been before, to question him about details and to ask for an expansion of his associations whenever it seemed necessary for a clearer grasp of the material he was presenting.

He now commenced a series of associations in which he emerged as sending various students for opinion to consultations with a specialist.

The next association I shall describe was the second of this kind: he said, "I have a student whose eye has been becoming affected. An eye man said he thought it was an infection. Anyway nothing could be done about it, but her father said he wanted another opinion. So I had to send her to another eye man and now I have got landed with a whole lot of work I don't want to do; she's a nuisance. I have to give a whole series of interviews. The second eye man doesn't think it's much different clinically from what the first eye man says, but he thinks it's worth doing something. The first man didn't think it worth bothering and that is why her father thought him a bit slack I suppose. Anyhow I have to do this now. She must get a blood test done to see if she has syphilis. She should have done it before".

24. This association may be considered as the starting point of an investigation which illuminated two problems: first, the unconscious material that it expressed and, second, the manner in which the patient was able to bring this material into consciousness.

As his analysis unfolded it was possible to demonstrate that his association, with its subsequent variations, compactly expressed the following themes:

1. I was the first eye man who said, in effect, that the

injured girl was an internal object, infected by the bad objects inside him, for which nothing could be done. I was also the second eye man who said that the injured girl was injured by his faeces, spirochaetes and bacilli, all varieties of bad penes, for whom nothing could be done but for whom he would have to do it just the same. He would have to cure her with his penis, since I would not repair damage done by him and it was his object in any case; and he would have to cure her without any pleasurable gain. I was also the eye surgeon who threatened him with castration. He had spent some anxious hours on correspondence to see that no question of jealousy or friction marred the relationship between the two eye men and between them and himself. So the twins were to be brought into harmonious co-operation.

2. The first, passive, eye man represented his previous psycho-therapeutic experiences which had left him and his objects more or less in peace. The second eye man was psycho-analysis that was giving him increased insight, and seducing him into genital sexuality and the threatening situation that went with it.

3. The first, passive, eye man was the mother and the second, active, eye man the father whom he tried to harmonize by his correspondence with both.

25. I will now consider the light his analysis threw on the second problem—the manner in which the patient brought this material into consciousness.

My first point is that with his association we are back again on the theme of contamination. The girl has an infection, be it tubercular, syphilitic, or obscure. He himself noted spontaneously that he had not mentioned, although in the actual case it had been canvassed, the possibility of diabetes. We were thus rehearsing a topic which had already been well tested, as it were orally, in the past $2\frac{1}{2}$ years of analysis, but which was now to be re-investigated by other means.

The consultation of two eye men indicated an occular method of investigation. Furthermore, a modification of the twin theme, the two eye men, was again in evidence.

26. The result of this re-investigation had been increase of hope, but also of fresh burdens and responsibilities; amongst

2

these was the possibility of genital sexuality, a further essay in the oral sexuality which he had neglected, withdrawal of blood, possibly contaminated, from the object, and the giving of injections.

The eye men, particularly the second, also represented the reinforcement of the investigating weapons by something like intellect: they were supposed to know more than himself.

Throughout this period it was clear that I was felt to be present and indeed my presence was even regarded as necessary. But I was not to interfere. Any interpretation which had in it the least tincture which my patient could interpret as an incursion into the realms of diagnosis and treatment was resented; but I could be myself, not just a twin to be fashioned into a shape he desired. If I observed the manifestations presented to me by my patient in the consulting room in terms of play therapy with a child then I could consider the two eye men as parts of his body, possibly his two eyes that were to be harmonized into binocular vision. The injured girl was some object, recovered from his inside, which was to be subjected to the scrutiny of both his eyes and a developing intellect, a scrutiny thus exercised on an externalized object.

The results of this scrutiny were not altogether reassuring, for one thing the two eye men were not completely harmonized, for another the diagnosis remained obscure, or, in other words, the intellect had not solved the problem, and finally, there had been foreshadowed the imposition of further and burdensome responsibilities, namely a revision of oral sexuality and an exploration of genital sexuality. At this last point, I noticed that he had begun to call the eye man an eye surgeon. When I drew his attention to this, he said the surgeon had not thought an operation necessary.

I was not surprised when at the next session another student had to be sent for a consultation, this time to an ear, nose and throat surgeon, and again at the request of the father. In recounting this episode, he expressed persecutory feelings towards the ear, nose and throat man. A retreat to auditory, olfactory and oral levels had taken place. I interpreted that his advance had been felt to be impossible to sustain and that he felt persecuted not only for the reasons already educed but also because psycho-analysis, a method that involved examining his problems with all his senses, including sight and intellect, was far more burdensome than psycho-therapy; it involved (1) painful co-ordination, which he had not been able to accomplish (2) the acceptance by himself of all the splittings of his personality which he had personified and externalized (3) the imposition of responsibilities which he could not shoulder and (4) the threatened punishment of castration which he could not sustain. I reminded him of the dream of the painter who presented too large a bill and said that I was thus the object of his hatred both because I was imposing on him these responsibilities and punishments and forcing him to retreat to levels which he had already found unendurable. I pointed out to him that it looked, since he said the ear, nose and throat surgeon had agreed that his treatment was correct, as if all levels indicated that he was responsible and should restore the injured object.

27. I told the patient that we must consider that the one component that remained unaltered whatever happened was his conscience and that this seemed so exacting that he was driven by it from one frightening and demanding situation to another.

The patient's oscillations helped him to try out his methods of reality testing by enabling him to compare his findings in oral and ocular phases. The injured object had been very thoroughly explored on an oral level before being submitted for scrutiny by the "eye men". Nevertheless the change to the eye men aroused great anxiety and tension because, instead of simply solving the problem of the injured object, they revealed the presence of the oedipus situation which he could not tolerate. The subsequent succession of advances and regressions served the purpose of enabling him to strengthen the ego; he could therefore deal with the oedipus situation, now become emotionally powerful which it never was before the emergence of the imaginary twin. I have already remarked on the way in which the analysis seemed to have no effect whatever on oedipal material of the early phase. At this point in his analysis there seemed to go together an increase of confidence in his methods of reality testing, in reality, and in his ego.

28. I have now completed my account of all the clinical material I propose to present from the analysis of this patient. In the discussion that follows I shall have to refer to associations from two other patients and in order to keep the material distinct I propose to call the patient of whom I have so far spoken, "A", and the other two "B" and "C" respectively.

The first point I would discuss is the mastery and confidence displayed by patient "A" in his use of the mechanisms of introjection, projection, splitting and the personification of his splits. His reactions contrasted, during the period I have described, with those of patient "B", a real twin and a more disturbed personality, who resorted to phantasies of an identical twin, phantasies which seemed intended to serve the same functions as "A"s imaginary twin. This patient seemed always to be struggling with the intractability of his material. Introjected objects were described as cubes of burnished steel: he complained during sessions of pain in mouth, stomach and anus. Sustenance had to be drawn through a hair-fine tube, and the associations by which he strove to obtain relief in analysis were tenuous and fitful to match. His real twin seemed as intractable as material for phantasy as food appeared to be for sustenance. Patient "A" personified his splits with such success that in some sessions, as I have said, one might almost imagine one's self watching a session of play therapy with a child. "B" seemed to feel as inadequately equipped for the exploration of intra-psychic tensions as he did for contact with reality and I could not help feeling that "A", particularly in the sessions devoted to the consultants, when he seemed able to tolerate my presence as a person in my own right, was demonstrating, by his personifications, his attempt to bridge the gulf to reality, and displaying, in doing so, one factor that contributed to hopefulness about the outcome of his analysis. In his testing of reality the patient was also testing, apparently with growing confidence in the results, his mechanisms for testing reality.

29. In this respect he seems to me to differ from patient "C" whose association which I shall now give indicated no such confidence either in reality or in his means for testing it. "C" told me, after returning to analysis from hospital where his treatment by deep X-ray therapy had been canvassed only to be rejected on the grounds that it might be dangerous on account of possible destruction of genital function, that he had been next to a patient who was being transfused with blood of which the donor was his cousin. The cousins had mothers who were twin sisters, he said, and added, reflectively, that his sister had twins. His doctor, he went on, had the same name as the doctor who had treated him some time previously when he had been abroad and suffered from indigestion. He paused; and then said one of his eyes was weak. Furthermore, if he used his eye alone he saw double. His defect in vision could be corrected with glasses but he hated wearing his glasses, which in fact did correct his sight, because they made him feel cross-eyed. I made the interpretation that the two cousins were parents in intercourse whom he wished to destroy with his penetrating, sadistic, X-ray gaze and that he felt in consequence that his genitality was menaced by the destructive scrutiny of the parents. He replied with an all-embracing pun, I am unreliable. No sooner had he said it than he began to complain of indigestion, expressed his fears of having to return to hospital and spent the rest of the session in fears about his food. This patient frequently complained that it was equally disturbing whether he concluded that his observations were correct, in which case the reality was terrifying, or whether he concluded they were incorrect, in which case his mental state was terrifying. His pun indicated that, unlike "A", he felt he could not rely on his instruments of investigation, the eye and all it stood for, the parents that his eye revealed, and the ego that had to incorporate the result of the investigation. He, like "A", regressed to an oral level.

30. I now turn to a session with the patient "B" whom I mentioned earlier. He said: "I saw your last patient I think. I came early and have been waiting. Last night my twin kept me up all night telling me some long-winded rigmarole the way these people do. I was wanting to go to my bed all the time. Thanks to psycho-analysis I can see right through the mind of the man who works at the next table to mine. I can laugh at him."

I interpreted that the twin was my last patient who had kept him out with his rigmarole. But he could laugh at him now as he knew what he must be feeling now he was excluded.

"B" went on, "My lab. man likes using the ordinary microscope but I prefer the binocular. There's no doubt at all you can see far better. Mind you he partly agrees with me. I've just been thinking how much better treatment you can get when you have more money and that of course makes you better."

I said psycho-analysis or myself gave him binocular vision. As a result he had more knowledge and increased knowledge was felt to bring healing.

He went on, "Life is very complicated. You just go and make things difficult for me."

I replied, "You are now feeling that the better vision that two eyes give you, analysis being one of them, shows you more than poor monocular vision; it makes you realize life is very complicated and difficult. It has made you see the other patient who comes to me."

He continued: "I could not eat my lunch. It looked very nice but it made me feel sick."

I replied, "Your eyes made you think when you saw the other patient was here that the analysis was very nice. Now you find it is poisoning you and you do not feel able to take it. There is a feeling that the other patient's rigmarole as you called it is something he has left behind to poison you."

He continued: "Of course the binocular microscope is very difficult to use at first. You have to learn how to use it and then it is much better than the ordinary one."

I replied, "You are feeling that if you use your analysis to see right through people to laugh at them you have not learned to use it properly and then others you look at attack you back again."

31. Subsequent analysis showed that the doubt he had

about his ability to use the binocular microscope straight away was partly based on his fear that it might make a very small twin look like a very big father. At the time of this association he was not prepared to see a father and a mother together although his association showed that such a scene might be revealed—if his instruments of investigation, and ability to use them, improved. This warning too was implicit in the statement that I made things very difficult for him. His claim that he possessed psycho-analytical insight indicated that I was in the role of the identical twin—this patient's imaginary twin.

The session I have described indicated to me that "B" had now reached a point where interpretations of myself as the identical twin had become possible. Up to this point oedipal material, though quite apparent was, as with "A" in the early phase, on a superficial level and interpretations had little effect. His statements about the need to become skilled in the use of the binocular microscope indicate a growing sense of reality towards his means of establishing contact and growing confidence in his ability to explore intra-psychic tensions, whereas all through the earlier part of his analysis I had come into the picture again and again as his brain that had to do his exploration for him, and this brings me to the next point I wish to discuss. How was it that with "A" the emergence of the imaginary twin was so important? And if it was so important, why had the phenomena associated with it remained peripheral and not central for so long?

The answer I suggest is that the imaginary twin goes back to his very earliest relationship and is an expression of his inability to tolerate an object that was not entirely under his control. The function of the imaginary twin was thus to deny a reality different from himself.

With this denial of external reality there co-existed his inability to tolerate the internal psychic realities and a great deal of work had to be done before any increase in tolerance occurred. As his fears of his psychic mechanisms decreased it became possible for him to allow their presence to manifest itself by a movement of their representation in his stream of associations into a more central position. Only when I had been able to demonstrate how bad I was on all levels of his mind did it become possible for him first to recognize his mechanisms of splitting and personification and then to employ them, as it were in reverse, to establish the contact which they had originally been used to break. After the demonstration of the imaginary twin I began to be allowed existence as a real person and not a thing created by himself until the point, already mentioned, when I felt I was allowed to exist more or less passively watching his play and finally as a consultant. In the session I have described with "B", despite some appearances to the contrary, I was still only an identical twin.

32. I have left till last two speculations which pose questions I do not propose to attempt to answer. The first concerns the personification of splits to which I have drawn attention. Is it possible that the capacity to personify splittings of the personality is in some way analogous to a capacity for symbol formation to which Mrs. Klein has drawn attention in her paper on "The Importance of Symbol-Formation in the Development of the Ego"; had it a similar value in the development of "A" in the period I have attempted to describe?

My second question is concerned with the part played by vision in these three patients' associations. In each of them it seems to be linked with the development of intellect, witness the consultant in "A", myself as the brain with "B", and in a similar role, though I had no time to bring it in, with "C", and in each with the emergence of genital sexuality and the oedipus situation. Furthermore, each patient in his individual way seemed to have similar problems that obtruded themselves almost as if concerned with vision itself. "A" stressed how much work he had thrust upon him to keep the relationship with the two eye men harmonious; "B" compared the merits of monocular and binocular microscopes; "C" the need for glasses to correct his sight. Each seemed to feel that new burdens had been imposed; "A" by the second eye man, "B" by myself making things difficult for him, and "C" by saying the glasses made him feel cross-eyed.

In each case I have mentioned, the visual power has represented the emergence of a new capacity for exploring the environment: it has been possible to show that in this respect the analysis was being felt as an addition to the patient's armoury for investigation and was likely therefore to be reactivating emotions associated with very early advances in psychological development that had a similar effect in increasing capacity. The increase of power was felt to demand an increase in intellectual grasp.

33. In each case the newly achieved powers were used to solve an already existing problem but were found to reveal still other problems that demanded solution. Thus "A", who seemed preoccupied with the problem of an internal injured object, and brought to bear on it his fresh powers, found himself threatened by the relationship between father and child. "B" showed the same development expressed in terms of the discovery of a by no means identical twin that had a relationship with a mother. "C" likewise—but in terms of a cousin being transfused with the blood of another.

All three patients seemed to feel that the problem had been there all the time but that its revelation had depended on increased capacity for awareness.

The regression in each case could thus be stated as being away from (1) the increase in capacity produced by psychological development (2) the phenomena brought into awareness by the increased capacity (3) the physiological development, associated with the psychological development which revealed the relationship between the external parents.

In each case I had the impression that the patient felt that sight produced problems of mastery of a new sense organ. This had its counterpart in a feeling that development of the psyche, like development of visual capacity, involved the emergence of the oedipus situation. With "A", the change from a perfunctory and superficial treatment of the oedipus situation to a struggle to come to terms with an emotionally charged oedipus complex was extremely striking.

For myself, I have found it impossible to interpret the material presented to me by these patients as a manifestation of purely psychological development divorced from any concurrent physical development. I have wondered whether the psychological development was bound up with the development of ocular control in the same way that problems of development linked with oral aggression co-exist with the eruption of teeth. If this is so, we would have to ask ourselves if these psychological developments, ushering in the oedipus complex, come close to the first four months in the individual's life. The relevance of this to assessment of the correctness or otherwise of Mrs. Klein's view of the earliness of the oedipal phase is obvious; if the experience of other observers appears to confirm my impressions it may provide incidental reasons for favouring an early date for the pre-oedipal phase.

3 Notes on the Theory of Schizophrenia[1]

A. Introduction

34. In this paper I shall discuss the schizophrenic patient's use of language and the bearing of this on the theory and practice of analysis. At a later date I shall acknowledge my indebtedness to, and discuss the views of, the psycho-analysts who have contributed to the growth of my own views. I cannot do that now, but I must make it clear for the better understanding of what I say that, even where I do not make specific acknowledgement of the fact, Melanie Klein's work occupies a central position in my view of the psycho-analytic theory of schizophrenia. I assume that the explanation of terms such as "projective identification" and the "paranoid" and "depressive positions" is known through her work.

By approaching the subject through consideration of verbal thought I run the risk of appearing to neglect the nature of the schizophrenic's object relations. I must therefore emphasize now that I think that the peculiarity of the schizophrenic's object relations is the oustanding feature of schizophrenia. The importance of the points that I wish to make lies in their capacity to illuminate the nature of this object relationship of which they are a subordinate function.

35. The material is derived from the analysis of six patients; two were drug addicts, one an obsessional anxiety state with schizoid features, and the remaining three schizophrenics all of whom suffered from hallucinations which were well in evidence over a period of between four and five years of analysis. Of these three, two showed marked paranoid features and one depression.

I did not depart from the psycho-analytic procedure I usually employ with neurotics, being careful always to take up both positive and negative aspects of the transference.

[1] Paper read in the Symposium "The Psychology of Schizophrenia" at the 18th International Psycho-Analytical Congress in London on 28 July, 1953.

B. Nature of the Observation on which Interpretations are Based

Evidence for interpretations has to be sought in the counter-transference and in the actions and free associations of the patient. Counter-transference has to play an important part in analysis of the schizophrenic, but I do not propose to discuss this to-day. I shall therefore pass on to the patient's free associations.

C. Schizophrenic Language

36. Language is employed by the schizophrenic in three ways; as a mode of action, as a method of communication, and as a mode of thought. He will show a preference for action on occasions when other patients would realize that what was required was thought; thus, he will want to go over to a piano to take out the movement to understand why someone is playing the piano. Reciprocally, if he has a problem the solution of which depends on action, as when, being in one place, he should be in another, he will resort to thought —omnipotent thought—as his mode of transport.

At the moment I want to consider only his use of it as a mode of action in the service either of splitting the object or projective identification. It will be noted that this is but one aspect of schizophrenic object relations in which he is either splitting or getting in and out of his objects.

The first of these uses is in the service of projective identification. In this the patient uses words as things or as split-off parts of himself which he pushes forcibly into the analyst. Typical of the consequences of this behaviour is the experience of a patient who felt he got inside me at the beginning of each session and had to be extricated at the end of it.

Language is again employed as a mode of action for the splitting of his object. This obtrudes when the analyst becomes identified with internal persecutors, but it is employed at other times too. Here are two examples of this use of language: The patient comes into the room, shakes me warmly by the hand, and looking piercingly into my eyes says, "I think the sessions are not for a long while but stop me ever going out." I know from previous experience that this patient has a grievance that the sessions are too few and that they interfere with his free time. He intended to split me by making me give two opposite interpretations at once, and this was shown by his next association when he said, "How does the lift know what to do when I press two buttons at once?"

My second example has wide implications, which I cannot take up here, because of their bearing on insomnia. The technique depends on the combination of two incompatible elements thus: the patient speaks in a drowsy manner calculated to put the analyst to sleep. At the same time he stimulates the analyst's curiosity. The intention is again to split the analyst, who is not allowed to go to sleep and is not allowed to keep awake.

You will note a third example of splitting later on when I describe a patient splitting the analyst's speech itself.

To turn now to the schizophrenic's difficulties with language as a mode of thought. Here is a sequence of associations all in one session, but separated from each other by intervals of four or five minutes.

I have a problem I am trying to work out.

As a child I never had phantasies.

I knew they weren't facts so I stopped them.

I don't dream nowadays.

Then after a pause he went on in a bewildered voice, "I don't know what to do now." I said, "About a year ago you told me you were no good at thinking. Just now you said you were working out a problem—obviously something you were thinking about."

Patient. "Yes." *Analyst.* "But you went on with the thought that you had no phantasies in childhood; and then that you had no dreams; you then said that you did not know what to do. It must mean that without phantasies and without dreams you have not the means with which to think out your problem." The patient agreed, and began to talk with marked freedom and coherence. The reference to the inhibition of phantasy as a severe disability hindering development supports Melanie Klein's observations in her paper "A Contribution to the Theory of Intellectual Inhibition".

37. The severe splitting in the schizophrenic makes it difficult for him to achieve the use of symbols and subsequently of substantives and verbs. It is necessary to demonstrate these difficulties to him as they arise; of this I shall shortly give an example. The capacity to form symbols is dependent on:

(1) The ability to grasp whole objects.

(2) The abandonment of the paranoid-schizoid position with its attendant splitting.

(3) The bringing together of splits and the ushering in of the depressive position.

Since verbal thought depends on the ability to integrate, it is not surprising to find that its emergence is intimately associated with the depressive position which, as Melanie Klein has pointed out, is a phase of active synthesis and integration. Verbal thought sharpens awareness of psychic reality and therefore of the depression which is linked with destruction and loss of good objects. The presence of internal persecutors, as another aspect of psychic reality, is similarly unconsciously more recognized. The patient feels that the association between the depressive position and verbal thought is one of cause and effect—itself a belief based on his capacity to integrate—and this adds one more to the many causes of his hatred, already well in evidence, of analysis, which is after all a treatment which employs verbal thought in the solution of mental problems.

The patient at this stage becomes frightened of the analyst, even though he may concede that he feels better, but, and this is where the kernel of our problem lies, he shows every sign of being anxious to have nothing whatever to do with his embryonic capacity for verbal thought. That is felt to be better left to the analyst; or, as I think it more correct to say, the analyst is felt to be better able than he to harbour it within himself without disaster. The patient seems, despite all the work done, to have reverted to the use of language that I have described as characteristic of the schizophrenic before analysis. He has greater verbal capacity but prefers to employ it as he did when it was slight.

D. Development of Capacity for Verbal Thought

38. To explain why the patient is so chary of using his increased capacity I must report an experience which seems to have peculiar significance for him. A patient said to me, "I am a prisoner of psycho-analysis"; later in the session he added, "I can't escape". Some months later he said, "I can't get out of my state of mind". A mass of material, to which quotations cannot do justice, had accumulated over a period of three years to give the impression that the patient felt unable to escape from a prison which seemed sometimes to be me, sometimes psycho-analysis and sometimes his state of mind which is a constant struggle with his own internal objects. He thus shows the same attitude to verbal thought as he has to his potency and his equipment for work and love.

The problem to which I am addressing myself can best be understood if it is seen to appertain to the moment when the patient feels he has effected his escape. The escape appears to contribute to the patient's feeling which he occasionally reports, that he is better; but it has cost him dear. The same patient said, "I have lost my words", and meant by this, as further analysis disclosed, that the instrument with which he had effected his escape had been lost in the process. Words, the capacity for verbal thought, the one essential for further progress, have gone. On expansion it appears that he thinks he has reached this pass as a penalty for forging this instrument of verbal thought and using it to escape from his former state of mind; hence the unwillingness I described to use his greater verbal capacity except as a mode of action.

Here now is the example I promised you when I was speaking of the difficulty that schizophrenic splitting caused in the formation of symbols and the development of verbal thought. The patient was a schizophrenic who had been in analysis five years; I describe some essentials of two sessions. I must warn you that compression has compelled me to leave out many repetitive formulations which in fact would mitigate the baldness of the interpretations as I report them here. I think interpretation should be in language that is simple, exact and mature.

Patient. I picked a tiny piece of skin from my face and feel quite empty.

Analyst. The tiny piece of skin is your penis, which you have torn out, and all your insides have come with it.

Patient. I do not understand . . . penis . . . only syllables.

Analyst. You have split my word "penis" into syllables and it now has no meaning.

Patient. I don't know what it means, but I want to say, "If I can't spell I cannot think".

Analyst. The syllables have now been split into letters; you cannot spell—that is to say you cannot put the letters together again to make words. So now you cannot think.

The patient started the next day's session with disjointed associations and complained that he could not think. I reminded him of the session I have described, whereupon he resumed correct speech; thus:

Patient. I cannot find any interesting food.

Analyst. You feel it has all been eaten up.

Patient. I do not feel able to buy any new clothes and my socks are a mass of holes.

Analyst. By picking out the tiny piece of skin yesterday you injured yourself so badly you cannot even buy clothes; you are empty and have nothing to buy them with.

Patient. Although they are full of holes they constrict my foot.

Analyst. Not only did you tear out your own penis but also mine. So to-day there is no interesting food—only a hole, a sock. But even this sock is made of a mass of holes, all of which you made and which have joined together to constrict, or swallow and injure, your foot.

This and subsequent sessions confirmed that he felt he had eaten the penis and that therefore there was no interesting food left, only a hole. But this hole was now so persecutory that he had to split it up. As a result of the splitting the hole became a mass of holes which all came together in a persecutory way to constrict his foot.

This patient's picking habits had been worked over for some three years. At first he had been occupied only with blackheads, and I shall quote from Freud's description of three cases, one observed by himself, one by Dr. Tausk and one by R. Reitler, which have a resemblance to my patient. They are taken from his paper on "The Unconscious" (1915).

Of his patient Freud said, "he has let himself withdraw from all the interests of life on account of the unhealthy condition of the skin of his face. He declares that he has blackheads and that there are deep holes in his face which everyone notices". Freud says he was working out his castration complex on his skin and that he began to think there was a deep cavity wherever he had got rid of a blackhead. He continues: "The cavity which then appears in consequence of his guilty act is the female genital, i.e. stands for the fulfilment of the threat of castration (or the phantasy representing it) called forth by onanism". Freud compares such substitute-formations with those of the hysteric, saying, "A tiny little hole such as a pore of the skin will hardly be used by an hysteric as a symbol for the vagina, which otherwise he will compare with every imaginable object capable of enclosing a space. Besides we should think that the multiplicity of these little cavities would prevent him from using them as a substitute for the female genital".

Of Tausk's case he says, "in pulling on his stockings he was disturbed by the idea that he must draw apart the knitted stitches, i.e. the holes, and every hole was for him a symbol of the female genital aperture".

Quoting Reitler's case he says the patient "found the explanation that his foot symbolized the penis; putting on the stocking stood for an onanistic act".

I shall now return to my patient at a session ten days later A tear welled from his eye and he said with a mixture of despair and reproach, "Tears come from my ears now".

This kind of association had by now become familiar to me, so I was aware that I had been set a problem in interpretation. But by this time the patient, who had been in analysis some six years, was capable of a fair degree of identification with the analyst and I had his help. I shall not attempt a description of the stages by which the conclusions I put before you were reached. The steps were laborious and slow even though we had the evidence of six years' analysis on which to draw.

It appeared that he was deploring a blunder that seemed to bear out his suspicion that his capacity for verbal communication was impaired. It seemed that his sentence was but another instance of an inability to put words together properly.

After this had been discussed it was seen that tears were very bad things, that he felt much the same about tears which came from his ears as he did about sweat that came from the holes in his skin when he had, as he supposed, removed blackheads or other such objects from the skin. His feeling about tears from his ears was seen to be similar to his feeling about the urine that came from the hole that was left in a person when his penis had been torn out; the bad urine still came.

When he told me that he couldn't listen very well I took advantage of his remark to remind him that in any case we needed to know why his mind was full of such thoughts at the present juncture, and I suggested that probably his hearing was felt to be defective because my words were being drowned by the tears that poured from his ears.

When it emerged that he couldn't talk very well either I suggested that it was because he felt his tongue had been torn out and he had been left only with an ear.

This was followed by what seemed to be a completely chaotic series of words and noises. I interpreted that now he felt he had a tongue but it was really just as bad as his ear—it just poured out a flow of destroyed language. In short it appeared that despite his wishes and mine we could not, or he felt we could not, communicate. I suggested that he felt he had a very bad and hostile object inside him which was treating our verbal intercourse to much the same kind of destructive attack which he had once felt he had launched against parental intercourse whether sexual or verbal.

At first he seemed to feel most keenly the defects in his

capacity for communication or thought, and there was a great deal of play with the pronunciation of tears (*teers* or *tares*) the emphasis being mostly on the inability to bring together the objects, words, or word pronunciation, except cruelly. But at one point he seemed to become aware that his association had been the starting-point for much discussion. Then, "Lots of people" he murmured. On working this out in turn it appeared that he had swung away from the idea that his verbal capacity was being irretrievably destroyed by the attacks to which our conversation was being subjected, to the idea that his verbal communication was extremely greedy. This greed was ministered to by his splitting himself into so many people that he could be in many different places at once to hear the many different interpretations which I, also split into "lots of people", was now able to give simultaneously instead of one by one. His greed, and the attacks on verbal communication by the internal persecutors, were therefore related to each other.

39. Clearly this patient felt that splitting had destroyed his ability to think. This was the more serious for him because he no longer felt that action provided a solution for the kind of problem with which he was struggling. This state is equated by the patient with "insanity".

The patient believes he has lost his capacity for verbal thought because he has left it behind inside his former state of mind, or inside the analyst, or inside psycho-analysis. He also believes that his capacity for verbal thought has been removed from him by the analyst who is now a frightening person. Both beliefs give rise to characteristic anxieties. The belief that he has left it behind has, as we have seen, helped to make the patient feel he is insane. He thinks that he will never be able to progress unless he goes back, as it were, into his former state of mind in order to fetch it. This he dare not do because he dreads his former state of mind and fears that he would once more be imprisoned in it. The belief that the analyst has removed his capacity for verbal thought makes the patient afraid of employing his new-found capacity for verbal thought, lest it should arouse the hatred of the analyst and cause him to repeat the attack.

From the patient's point of view the achievement of verbal thought has been a most unhappy event. Verbal thought is so interwoven with catastrophe and the painful emotion of depression that the patient, resorting to projective identification, splits it off and pushes it into the analyst. The results are again unhappy for the patient; lack of this capacity is now felt by him to be the same thing as being insane. On the other hand, reassumption of this capacity seems to him to be inseparable from depression and awareness, on a reality level this time, that he is "insane". This fact tends to give reality to the patient's phantasies of the catastrophic results that would accrue were he to risk re-introjection of his capacity for verbal thought.

It must not be supposed that the patient leaves his problems untouched during this phase. He will occasionally give the analyst concrete and precise information about them. The analyst's problem is the patient's dread, now quite manifest, of attempting a psycho-analytic understanding of what they mean for him, partly because the patient now understands that psycho-analysis demands from him that very verbal thought which he dreads.

So far I have dealt with the problem of communication between analyst and schizophrenic patient. I shall now consider the experience the patient has when he lives through the process of achieving sufficient mastery of language to emerge from the "prison of psycho-analysis", or state of mind in which he previously felt himself to be hopelessly enclosed. The patient is apparently unaware of any existence outside the consulting room; there is no report of any external activity. There is merely an existence away from the analyst of which nothing is known except that he is "all right" or "better" and a relationship with the analyst which the patient says is bad. The intervals between sessions are admitted and feared. He complains that he is insane, expresses his fear of hallucination and delusion, and is extremely cautious in his behaviour lest he should become insane.

The living through of the emotions belonging to this phase leads to a shift towards higher valuation of the external object at the expense of the hallucinated internal object. This depends on the analysis of the patient's hallucinations and his insistence on allotting to real objects a subordinate role. If this has been done the analyst sees before him the ego and more normal object relations in process of development. I am assuming that there has been an adequate working through of the processes of splitting and the underlying persecutory anxiety as well as of reintegration. Herbert Rosenfeld has described some of the dangers of this phase. My experiences confirm his findings. I have observed the progress from multiple splits to four and from four to two and the great anxiety as integration proceeds with the tendency to revert to violent disintegration. This is due to intolerance of the depressive position, internal persecutors, and verbal thought. If splitting has been adequately worked through the tendency to split the object and the ego at the same time is kept within bounds. Each session is then a step in ego development.

E. Realization of Insanity

40. One of the penalties of attempting to clarify the complex phenomena of the schizophrenic patient's relationship with his objects is that if the attempt is successful it is delusively misleading. I would now redress the balance by approaching the phenomena I have already described from a rather different angle. I wish to take up the story at the point at which the splits are brought together, the patient escapes from his state of mind and the depressive position is ushered in. In particular I wish to draw attention to this concatenation of events when it is suffused by the illumination achieved through the development of a capacity for verbal thought. I have made it clear that this is a most important turning-point in the whole analysis. You may therefore have formed the impression that at this point the analysis enters into calm waters. It is necessary therefore that I should leave you with no illusions about this.

What takes place, if the analyst has been reasonably successful, is a realization by the patient of psychic reality; he realizes that he has hallucinations and delusions, may feel unable to take food, and have difficulty with sleep. The patient will direct powerful feelings of hatred towards the analyst. He will state categorically that he is insane and will express with intense conviction and hatred that it is the analyst who has driven him to this pass. The analyst ought to expect concern for the patient's welfare to drive the family to intervene and he must be prepared to explain an alarming situation to them. He should strive to keep at bay surgeons and shock therapists alike while concentrating on not allowing the patient for a single moment to retreat either from his realization that he is insane or from his hatred of the analyst who has succeeded, after so many years, in bringing him to an emotional realization of the facts that he has spent his whole life trying to evade. This may be the more difficult because, when the first panic begins to subside, the patient himself will begin to suggest that he feels better. Due weight must be given to this, but care must be taken to prevent its being used to delay investigation in detail of the ramifications in the analytic situation of the changes brought about in the patient's object relationships by the realization of his insanity.

F. Results

41. I am not yet prepared to offer any opinion about the prospects of treatment except to say that two of the three schizophrenics of whom I am speaking are now earning their living. I believe that if the course I have indicated above is followed there is reason to anticipate that the schizophrenic may achieve his own form of adjustment to reality which may be no less worthy of the title of "cure" because it is not of the same kind as that which is achieved by less disordered patients. I repeat that I do not think that any cure, however limited, will be achieved if, at the point I have tried to describe to you, the analyst attempts to reassure the patient and so undoes all the good work that has led to the latter's being able to realize the severity of his condition. At this point an opportunity, which must not be lost, has been created for exploring with the patient what it means to do analystic or any other kind of work when insane.

The experiences I have described to you compel me to conclude that at the onset of the infantile depressive position, elements of verbal thought increase in intensity and depth. In consequence the pains of psychic reality are exacerbated by it and the patient who regresses to the paranoid-schizoid position will, as he does so, turn destructively on his embryonic capacity for verbal thought as one of the elements which have led to his pain.

4 Development of Schizophrenic Thought[1]

42. In this paper, which must be regarded as a preliminary announcement, I do three things:

(i) I discuss the point at which the psychotic personality diverges from the non-psychotic; (ii) I examine the nature of that divergence; and (iii) I consider the consequences of it. Experience at the Congress at Geneva showed that the attempt to give clinical illustrations in a paper as compressed as this produced far more obscurity than illumination. This version is accordingly restricted to theoretical description.

The conclusions I arrive at were forged in analytic contact with schizophrenic patients and have been tested by me in practice. That I arrived at some degree of clarification, I owe mainly to three pieces of work. As they occupy a key position in this paper I shall remind you of them.

First: Freud's description, which I referred to in my paper at the London Congress of 1953, of the mental apparatus called into activity by the demands of the reality principle and in particular of that part of it which is concerned with conscious awareness of sense impressions. Second: Freud's tentative suggestion, in *Civilization and its Discontents*, of the importance of the conflict between life and death instincts. The point was taken up and developed by Melanie Klein, but Freud seemed to recede from it. Melanie Klein believes that this conflict persists throughout life, and this view I believe to be of great importance to an understanding of the schizophrenic. Third: Melanie Klein's description of the phantasied sadistic attacks that the infant makes on the breast during the paranoid-schizoid phase, and her discovery of Projective Identification. Projective Identification is a splitting off by the patient of a part of his personality and a projection of it into the object where it

[1] *International Journal of Psycho-Analysis*, Vol. 37, Parts 4–5, 1956.

becomes installed, sometimes as a persecutor, leaving the psyche from which it has been split off correspondingly impoverished.

Schizophrenic disturbance springs from an interaction between (i) the environment, and (ii) the personality. In this paper I ignore the environment and focus attention on four essential features of schizophrenic personality. First is a preponderance of destructive impulses so great that even the impulses to love are suffused by them and turned to sadism. Second is a hatred of reality which, as Freud pointed out, is extended to all aspects of the psyche that make for awareness of it. I add hatred of internal reality and all that makes for awareness of it. Third, derived from these two, is an unremitting dread of imminent annihilation. Fourth is a precipitate and premature formation of object relations, foremost amongst which is the transference, whose thinness is in marked contrast to the tenacity with which it is maintained. The prematurity, thinness, and tenacity are pathognomic and are alike derived from dread of annihilation by the death instincts. The schizophrenic is preoccupied with the conflict, never finally resolved, between destructiveness on the one hand and sadism on the other.

Transference

The relationship with the analyst is premature, precipitate, and intensely dependent. When the patient broadens it under pressure of his life or death instincts two concurrent streams of phenomena become manifest: First projective identification, with the analyst as object, becomes overactive with the resulting painful confusional states such as Rosenfeld has described. Second, the mental and other activities by which the dominant impulse, be it life instincts or death instincts, strives to express itself, are at once subjected to mutilation by the temporarily subordinated impulse. Driven by the wish to escape the confusional states and harassed by the mutilations, the patient strives to restore the restricted relationship; the transference is again invested with its characteristic featurelessness. Whether the patient walks straight past me into the consulting room as if scarcely aware of my presence, or whether he displays an effusive, mirthless bonhomie, the restricted relationship is unmistakable. Restriction and expansion alternate throughout the analysis.

The Divergence

43. To sum up; ignoring the effect of the external environment, the schizophrenic personality depends on the existence in the patient of four features; (i) a conflict that is never decided between life and death instincts; (ii) a preponderance of destructive impulses; (iii) hatred of external and internal reality; (iv) a tenuous but tenacious object relationship. This peculiar endowment makes it certain that the schizophrenic patient's progression through the paranoid-schizoid and depressive positions is markedly different from that of the non-psychotic personality. This difference hinges on the fact that this combination of characteristics leads to a massive resort to projective identification. It is therefore to projective identification that I now turn, *but my examination of it is restricted to its deployment by the schizophrenic against all that apparatus of awareness that Freud described as being called into activity by the demands of the reality principle.*

Divergence of Psychotic from Non-psychotic Personality

44. I spoke of Melanie Klein's picture of the paranoid-schizoid position and the important part played in it by the infant's phantasies of sadistic attacks on the breast. Identical attacks are directed against the apparatus of perception from the beginning of life. This part of his personality is cut up, split into minute fragments, and then, using the projective identification, expelled from the personality. Having thus rid himself of the apparatus of conscious awareness of internal and external reality, the patient achieves a state which is felt to be neither alive nor dead.

This apparatus of conscious awareness is intimately connected with verbal thought and all that provides, at the early stage of which I speak, the foundations of its inchoation.

Projective identification of conscious awareness and the

associated inchoation of verbal thought is the central factor in the differentiation of the psychotic from the non-psychotic personality. I believe it takes place at the outset of the patient's life. These sadistic attacks on the ego and on the foundations of inchoate verbal thought, and the projective identification of the fragments, makes certain that from this point on there is an ever-widening divergence between the psychotic and non-psychotic parts of the personality until at last the gulf is felt to be unbridgeable.

Fate of the Expelled Fragments

45. In so far as the destruction is successful, the patient experiences a failure in his capacity for perception. All his sense impressions appear to have suffered mutilation of a kind which would be appropriate had they been attacked as the breast is felt to be attacked in the sadistic phantasies of the infant. The patient feels imprisoned in the state of mind he has achieved and unable to escape from it because he feels he lacks the apparatus of awareness of reality, which is both the key to escape and the freedom itself to which he would escape. This sense of imprisonment is intensified by the menacing presence of the expelled fragments within whose planetary movements he is contained. The nature of this imprisonment will become clearer with the discussion of the fate of these expelled fragments, to which I now turn.

In the patient's phantasy the expelled particles of ego lead to an independent and uncontrolled existence outside the personality, but either containing or contained by external objects, where they exercise their functions as if the ordeal to which they have been subjected has served only to increase their number and to provoke their hostility to the psyche that ejected them. In consequence the patient feels himself to be surrounded by bizarre objects whose nature I shall now describe.

The Particles

46. Each particle is felt to consist of a real external object which is incapsulated in a piece of personality that has engulfed it. The character of this complete particle will

depend partly on the character of the real object, say a gramophone, and partly on the character of the particle of personality that engulfs it. If the piece of the personality is concerned with sight, the gramophone when played is felt to be watching the patient. If with hearing, then the gramophone when played is felt to be listening to the patient. The object, angered at being engulfed, swells up, so to speak, and suffuses and controls the piece of personality that engulfs it: to that extent the particle is felt to have become a thing. Since these particles are used by the patient as if they were prototypes of ideas—later to become words—this suffusion of the piece of personality by the contained, but controlling, object leads the patient to feel that words are the actual things they name, and so to the confusions, described by Segal, that arise because the patient equates, but does not symbolize.

Consequences for the Patient

47. The patient now moves, not in a world of dreams, but in a world of objects which are ordinarily the furniture of dreams. These objects, primitive yet complex, partake of qualities which in the non-psychotic are peculiar to matter, anal objects, senses, ideas, superego, and the remaining qualities of personality. One result is that the patient strives to use real objects as ideas and is baffled when they obey the laws of natural science and not those of mental functioning.

Associated with projective identification is the psychotic personality's inability to introject. If he wishes to take in an interpretation, or bring back these objects I have been describing, he does so by projective identification reversed, and by the same route. This situation was neatly summed up by the patient who said he used his intestine as a brain. When I said he had swallowed something, he replied, "The intestine doesn't swallow." Dr. Segal has described in her paper, which I had the good fortune to see before the Congress, some of the patient's vicissitudes in the depressive position; I would now add that, thanks to this employment of projective identification, he cannot synthesize his objects: he can only agglomerate and compress them. Further, whether he feels he has had something put into him, or whether he feels he has introjected it, he feels the ingress as an assault, and a retaliation by the object for his violent intrusion into it.

Repression

48. It will be clear that where the non-psychotic personality, or part of the personality, employs repression the psychotic has employed projective identification. Therefore there is no repression, and what should be his unconscious is replaced by the world of dream furniture in which I have described him as moving.

Verbal Thought

49. The inception of verbal thought which I described as appertaining to the depressive position is gravely disturbed because it is that which synthesizes and articulates impressions and thus is essential to awareness of internal and external reality; for that reason it is subject to continuing attacks such as I have described.

Further, excessive projective identification in the paranoid-schizoid position prevented smooth introjection and assimilation of sense impressions and consequently the establishment of the firm base of good objects on which the inception of verbal thought depends.

An attempt to think involves bringing back to control, and therefore to his personality, the expelled particles and their accretions. Projective identification is therefore reversed and the concomitant agglomeration and compression lead to highly compact speech, the construction of which is more appropriate to music than the articulation of words as used for non-psychotic communication.

Moreover, since, as we have seen, these particles share the qualities of things, the patient can feel he is being split by their re-entry. Again, since these particles include pieces of conscious awareness of sense impressions, the senses are felt to become painfully compressed and acute to an intolerable degree. The patient can be seen to be in the grip of extremely painful, tactile, auditory, or visual hallucinations. Depression and anxiety being subject to the same mechanism are similarly intensified till the patient is compelled to deal with these emotions in the way that Segal has described.

Conclusion

50. Experience of these theories in practice has convinced me that the treatment of psychotic personality will not be successful until the patient's destructive attacks on his ego, and his substitution of projective identification for repression and introjection, have been worked through. I further consider that even in the severe neurotic there is a psychotic personality that has to be dealt with in the same way before success is achieved.

5 Differentiation of the Psychotic from the Non-Psychotic Personalities[1]

51. The theme of this paper is that the differentiation of the psychotic from the non-psychotic personalities depends on a minute splitting of all that part of the personality that is concerned with awareness of internal and external reality, and the expulsion of these fragments so that they enter into or engulf their objects. I shall describe this process in some detail and shall then discuss its consequences and how they affect treatment.

The conclusions were arrived at in analytic contact with schizophrenic patients and have been tested by me in practice. I ask your attention for them because they have led to developments in my patients which are analytically significant and not to be confused, either with the remissions familiar to psychiatrists, or with that class of improvement that it is impossible to relate to the interpretations given or to any coherent body of psycho-analytic theory. I believe that the improvements I have seen deserve psycho-analytic investigation.

52. I owe my clarification of the obscurity that pervades the whole of a psychotic analysis mainly to three pieces of work. As they are crucial for understanding what follows I shall remind you of them. First: (2) Freud's description, referred to by me in my paper to the London Congress of 1953 (1), of the mental apparatus called into activity by the demands of the reality principle and in particular of that part of it which is concerned with the consciousness attached to the sense-organs. Second: Melanie Klein's (5) description of the phantasied sadistic attacks that the infant makes on the breast during the paranoid-schizoid phase, and third: her discovery of projective identification (7). By this mechanism the patient splits off a part of his personality and projects it into the object where it becomes installed,

[1] *International Journal of Psycho-Analysis*, Vol. 38, Parts 3–4, 1957.

sometimes as a persecutor, leaving the psyche, from which it has been split off, correspondingly impoverished.

53. Lest it be supposed that I attribute the development of schizophrenia exclusively to certain mechanisms apart from the personality that employs them, I shall enumerate now what I think are the preconditions for the mechanisms on which I wish to focus your attention. There is the environment, which I shall not discuss at this time, and the personality, which must display four essential features. These are: a preponderance of destructive impulses so great that even the impulse to love is suffused by them and turned to sadism; a hatred of reality, internal and external, which is extended to all that makes for awareness of it; a dread of imminent annihilation (7) and, finally, a premature and precipitate formation of object relations, foremost amongst which is the transference, whose thinness is in marked contrast with the tenacity with which they are maintained. The prematurity, thinnness and tenacity are pathognomonic and have an important derivation, in the conflict, never decided in the schizophrenic, between the life and death instincts.

54. Before I consider the mechanisms that spring from these characteristics I must dispose briefly of a few points that concern the transference. The relationship with the analyst is premature, precipitate, and intensely dependent; when under pressure of his life and death instincts, the patient broadens the contact, two concurrent streams of phenomena become manifest. First, splitting of his personality and projection of the fragments into the analyst (i.e. projective identification) becomes overactive, with consequent confusional states such as Rosenfeld (9) has described. Second, the mental and other activities by which the dominant impulse, be it of life or death instincts, strives to express itself, are at once subjected to mutilation by the temporarily subordinated impulse. Harassed by the mutilations and striving to escape the confusional states, the patient returns to the restricted relationship. Oscillation between the attempt to broaden the contact and the attempt to restrict continues throughout the analysis.

55. To return now to the characteristics I listed as intrinsic

to the schizophrenic personality. These constitute an endowment that makes it certain that the possessor of it will progress through the parnoid-schizoid and depressive positions in a manner markedly different from that of one not so endowed. The difference hinges on the fact that this combination of qualities leads to minute fragmentation of the personality, particularly of the apparatus of awareness of reality which Freud described as coming into operation at the behest of the reality principle, and excessive projection of these fragments of personality into external objects.

I described some aspects of these theories in my paper to the International Congress of 1953 (1) when I was speaking of the association of the depressive position with the development of verbal thought and the significance of this association for awareness of internal and external reality. In this paper I am taking up the same story only at a much earlier stage, namely at the outset of the patient's life. I am dealing with phenomena in the paranoid-schizoid position which are associated, ultimately, with the inchoation of verbal thought. How this should be so will, I hope, presently emerge.

56. The theories of Freud and Melanie Klein to which I referred earlier must now be considered in more detail. Quoting his formulation in his paper on "Neurosis and Psychosis" in 1924, Freud defined one of the features distinguishing the neuroses from the psychoses as: "in the former the ego, in virtue of its allegiance to reality, suppresses a part of the id (the life of instinct), whereas in the psychoses the same ego in the service of the id, withdraws itself from a part of reality" (4). I assume that when Freud speaks of the allegiance of the ego to reality he is speaking of the developments he described as taking place with the institution of the reality principle. He said, "the new demands made a succession of adaptations necessary in the mental apparatus, which, on account of insufficient knowledge, we can only detail very cursorily". He then lists: the heightened significance of the sense organs directed towards the outer world and of the consciousness attached to them; attention, which he calls a special function, which had to search the outer world in order that its data might be already familiar if an urgent inner need should arise; a system of notation whose task was to deposit the results of this periodical activity of consciousness which he describes as a part of that which we call memory; judgement which had to decide whether a particular idea was true or false; the employment of motor discharge in appropriate alteration of reality and not simply in unburdening the mental apparatus of accretions of stimuli; and, finally, thought which he says made it possible to tolerate the frustration which is an inevitable accompaniment of action by virtue of its quality as an experimental way of acting. As will be seen I very much extend the function and importance of thought, but otherwise accept the classification of ego function, which Freud put forward as putative, as giving concreteness to a part of the personality with which this paper is concerned. It accords well with clinical experience and illuminates events which I should have found infinitely more obscure without it.

I would make two modifications in Freud's description to bring it into closer relation with the facts. I do not think, at least as touches those patients likely to be met with in analytic practice, that the ego is ever wholly withdrawn from reality. I would say that its contact with reality is masked by the dominance, in the patient's mind and behaviour, of an omnipotent phantasy that is intended to destroy either reality or the awareness of it, and thus to achieve a state that is neither life nor death. Since contact with reality is never entirely lost, the phenomena which we are accustomed to associate with the neuroses are never absent and serve to complicate the analysis, when sufficient progress has been made, by their presence amidst psychotic material. On this fact, that the ego retains contact with reality, depends the existence of a non-psychotic personality parallel with, but obscured by, the psychotic personality.

57. My second modification is that the withdrawal from reality is an illusion, not a fact, and arises from the deployment of projective identification against the mental apparatus listed by Freud. Such is the dominance of this phantasy that it is evident that it is no phantasy, but a fact, to the patient, who acts as if his perceptual apparatus could

be split into minute fragments and projected into his objects.

As a result of these modifications we reach the conclusion that patients ill enough, say, to be certified as psychotic, contain in their psyche part of the personality, a prey to the various neurotic mechanisms with which psycho-analysis has made us familiar, and a psychotic part of the personality, which is so far dominant that the non-psychotic part of the personality, with which it exists in negative juxtaposition, is obscured.

One concomitant of the hatred of reality that Freud remarked is the psychotic infant's phantasies of sadistic attacks on the breast which Melanie Klein described as a part of the paranoid-schizoid phase (7). I wish to emphasize that in this phase the psychotic splits his objects, and contemporaneously all that part of his personality, which would make him aware of the reality he hates, into exceedingly minute fragments, for it is this that contributes materially to the psychotic's feelings that he cannot restore his objects or his ego. As a result of these splitting attacks, all those features of the personality which should one day provide the foundation for intuitive understanding of himself and others are jeopardized at the outset. All the functions which Freud described as being, at a later stage, a developmental response to the reality principle, that is to say, consciousness of sense impressions, attention, memory, judgement, thought, have brought against them, in such inchoate forms as they may possess at the outset of life, the sadistic splitting eviscerating attacks that lead to their being minutely fragmented and then expelled from the personality to penetrate, or encyst, the objects. In the patient's phantasy the expelled particles of ego lead an independent and uncontrolled existence, either contained by or containing the external objects; they continue to exercise their functions as if the ordeal to which they have been subjected had served only to increase their number and provoke their hostility to the psyche that ejected them. In consequence the patient feels himself to be surrounded by bizarre objects whose nature I shall now describe.

58. Each particle is felt to consist of a real object which is encapsulated in a piece of personality that has engulfed it. The nature of this complete particle will depend partly on the character of the real object, say a gramophone, and partly on the character of the particle of personality that engulfs it. If the piece of personality is concerned with sight, the gramophone when played is felt to be watching the patient; if with hearing, then the gramophone when played is felt to be listening to the patient. The object, angered at being engulfed, swells up, so to speak, and suffuses and controls the piece of personality that engulfs it: to that extent the particle of personality has become a thing. Since these particles are what the patient depends on for use as the prototypes of ideas—later to form the matrix from which words should spring—this suffusion of the piece of personality by the contained but controlling object leads the patient to feel that words are the actual things they name and so adds to the confusions, described by Segal, that arise because the patient equates, but does not symbolize. The fact that the patient uses these bizarre objects for achieving thought leads now to a fresh problem. If we consider that one of the patient's objects in using splitting and projective identification is to rid himself of awareness of reality it is clear that he could achieve the maximum of severance from reality with the greatest economy of effort if he could launch these destructive attacks on the link, whatever it is, that connects sense impressions with consciousness. In my paper to the 1953 International Congress (1) I showed that awareness of psychic reality depended on the development of a capacity for verbal thought the foundation of which was linked with the depressive position. It is impossible to go into this now. I refer you to Melanie Klein's 1930 paper on "The Importance of Symbol-formation in the Development of the Ego" (6) and to the paper given to the British Psychological Society (1955) by H. Segal (10). In this, Segal demonstrates the importance of symbol formation and explores its relationship to verbal thought and the reparative drives normally associated with the depressive position. I am concerned with an earlier stage in the same story. It is my belief that the mischief that becomes much more apparent in the depressive position has in fact been initiated in the paranoid-schizoid phase when the foundations for primitive thought should be laid, but are not, because of the overaction of splitting and projective identification.

59. Freud attributes to thought the function of providing a means of restraint of action. But he goes on to say, "It is probable that thinking was originally unconscious, in so far as it rose above mere ideation and turned to the relations between the object-impressions, and that it became endowed with further qualities which were perceptible to consciousness only through its connection with the memory traces of words" (2). My experiences have led me to suppose that some kind of thought, related to what we should call ideographs and sight rather than to words and hearing, exists at the outset. This thought depends on a capacity for balanced introjection and projection of objects and, a fortiori, on awareness of them. This is within the capacity of the non-psychotic part of the personality, partly because of the splitting and ejection of the apparatus of awareness I have already described and partly for reasons I am coming to now.

Thanks to the operations of the non-psychotic part of the personality the patient is aware that introjection is leading to the formation of the unconscious thought of which Freud speaks as "turned to the relations between object-impressions" I believe that it is this unconscious thought which Freud describes as turned to the relations between the object impressions which is responsible for the "consciousness attached to" the sense impressions. I am fortified in this belief by his statement twelve years later in the paper on "The Ego and the Id". In this he says "that the question 'How does a thing become conscious?' could be put more advantageously thus: 'How does a thing become preconscious?' And the answer would be: 'By coming into connection with the verbal images that correspond to it.' " (3). In my 1953 paper I said that verbal thought is bound up with awareness of psychic reality (1); this I also believe to be true of the early pre-verbal thought of which I am now speaking. In view of what I have already said of the psychotic's attacks on all that mental apparatus that leads to consciousness of external and internal reality, it is to be expected that the deployment of projective identification would be particularly severe against the thought, of whatsoever kind, that turned to the relations between object-impressions, for if this link could be severed, or better still never forged, then at least consciousness of reality would be destroyed even though reality itself could not be. But in fact the work of destruction is already half done as the material from which thought is forged, in the non-psychotic by balanced introjection and projection, is not available to the psychotic part of the personality, because the displacement of projection and introjection by projective identification has left him only with the bizarre objects I have described.

60. In fact, not only is primitive thought attacked because it links sense-impressions of reality with consciousness but, thanks to the psychotic's over-endowment with destructiveness, the splitting processes are extended to the links within the thought processes themselves. As Freud's phrase regarding thought being turned to the relations between object-impressions implies, this primitive matrix of ideographs from which thought springs contains within itself links between one ideograph and another. All these are now attacked till finally two objects cannot be brought together in a way which leaves each object with its intrinsic qualities intact and yet able, by their conjunction, to produce a new mental object. Consequently the formation of symbols, which depends for its therapeutic effect on the ability to bring together two objects so that their resemblance is made manifest, yet their difference left unimpaired, now becomes difficult. At a still later stage the result of these splitting attacks is seen in the denial of articulation as a principle for the combining of words. This last does not mean that objects cannot be brought together; as I shall show later when speaking of agglomeration, that is by no means true. Further, since that-which-links has been not only minutely fragmented but also projected out into objects to join the other bizarre objects, the patient feels surrounded by minute links which, being impregnated now with cruelty, link objects together cruelly.

To conclude my description of the fragmentation of the ego and its expulsion into and about its objects, I shall say that I believe the processes I have described to be the central factor, in so far as such a factor can be isolated without distortion, in the differentiation of the psychotic from the non-psychotic part of the personality. It takes place at the outset of the patient's life. The sadistic attacks on the ego and on the matrix of thought, together with projective identification of the fragments, make it certain that from this point on there is an ever-widening divergence between the psychotic and non-psychotic parts of the personality until at last the gulf between them is felt to be unbridgeable.

61. The consequences for the patient are that he now moves, not in a world of dreams, but in a world of objects which are ordinarily the furniture of dreams. His sense impressions appear to have suffered mutilation of a kind which would be appropriate had they been attacked as the breast is felt to be attacked in the sadistic phantasies of the infant (5). The patient feels imprisoned in the state of mind he has achieved, and unable to escape from it because he feels he lacks the apparatus of awareness of reality which is both the key to escape and the freedom to which he would escape. The sense of imprisonment is intensified by the menacing presence of the expelled fragments within whose planetary movements he is contained. These objects, primitive yet complex, partake of qualities which in the non-psychotic personality are peculiar to matter, anal objects, senses, ideas and superego.

62. The diversity of such objects, dependent as it is on the sense by which they are suffused, prevents more than the cursory indication of their mode of genesis that I have given. The reaction of these objects to material for ideographic thought leads the patient to confound real objects with primitive ideas and therefore to confusion when they obey the laws of natural science and not those of mental functioning. If he wishes to bring back any of these objects in an attempt at restitution of the ego, and in analysis he feels impelled to make the attempt, he has to bring them back by projective identification in reverse and by the route by which they were expelled. Whether he feels he has had one of these objects put into him by the analyst or whether he feels he had taken it in, he feels the ingress as an assault. The extreme degree to which he has carried the splitting of objects and ego alike makes any attempt at synthesis hazardous. Furthermore, as he has rid himself of that-which-joins, his capacity for articulation, the methods available for synthesis are felt to be macilent; he can compress but cannot join, he can fuse but cannot articulate. The capacity to join is felt, as a result of its ejection, to have become, like all other expelled particles, infinitely worse than they were when ejected. Any joining that takes place is done with a vengeance, that is to say in a manner expressly contrary to the wishes of the patient at the moment. In the course of the analysis this process of compression or agglomeration loses some of its malignancy and then fresh problems arise.

63. I must now draw your attention to a matter that demands a paper to itself and therefore cannot be more than mentioned here. It is implicit in my description that the psychotic personality or part of the personality has used splitting and projective identification as a substitute for repression. Where the non-psychotic part of the personality resorts to repression as a means of cutting off certain trends in the mind both from consciousness and from other forms of manifestation and activity, the psychotic part of the personality has attempted to rid itself of the apparatus on which the psyche depends to carry out the repressions; the unconscious would seem to be replaced by the world of dream furniture.

64. I shall now attempt a description of an actual session; it is a clinical experience based on these theories rather than the description of an experience on which the theories are based, but I hope I shall be able to indicate the material from previous sessions which led me to interpret as I did.

The patient at the time of this session, of which I describe a small part, had been coming to me for six years. He had once been as late as forty-five minutes, but had never missed a session; the sessions were never continued over time. On this morning he arrived a quarter of an hour late and lay on the couch. He spent some time turning from one side to another, ostensibly making himself comfortable. At length he said, "I don't suppose I shall do anything today. I ought to have rung up my mother." He paused and then said: "No; I thought it would be like this." A more prolonged pause followed; then, "Nothing but filthy things and smells", he said. "I think I've lost my sight". Some twenty-five minutes of our time had now passed, and at this point I made an interpretation, but before I repeat it I must discuss some previous material which will, I hope, make my intervention comprehensible.

When the patient was manoeuvring on the couch I was watching something with which I was familiar. Five years earlier he had explained that his doctor advised an operation for hernia and it was to be assumed that the discomfort caused by the hernia compelled these adjustments. It was, however, evident that more was involved than the hernia and rational activity to increase his physical comfort. I had sometimes asked him what these movements were, and to these questions his reply had been, "Nothing". Once he had said, "I don't know". I had felt that "Nothing" was a thinly veiled invitation to me to mind my own business as well as a denial of something very bad. I continued, over the weeks and years, to watch his movements. A handkerchief was disposed near his right pocket; he arched his back—surely a sexual gesture here? A lighter fell out of his pocket. Should he pick it up? Yes. No. perhaps not. Well, yes. It was retrieved from the floor and placed by the handkerchief. Immediately a shower of coins spilled over the couch on to the floor. The patient lay still and waited. Perhaps, his gesture seemed to suggest, he had been unwise to bring back the lighter. It had seemed to lead to the shower of coins. He waited, cautiously, furtively. And finally he made the remark I have reported. It reminded me of his descriptions, not given in any one session but produced over many months, of the tortuous manoeuvres through which he had to go before he went to the lavatory, or went down to breakfast, or telephoned to his mother. I was quite used to recalling many of the free associations which might easily be appropriate to the behaviour he displayed on this as on many other mornings. But these were now my associations, and once when I had tried to make use of such material in an interpretation that is exactly the reply he had made. One interpretation I remembered which had met with some success. I had pointed out that he felt much the same about these movements as he had about a dream he had told me—he had no ideas about the dream and he had no ideas about the movements. "Yes", he had agreed, "that's so". "And yet", I replied, "you once had an idea about it; you thought it was the hernia". "That's nothing", he replied, and had then paused, almost slyly I thought, to see if I had grasped the point. So, "Nothing is really a hernia", I said. "No idea", he replied, "only a hernia." I had been left feeling that his "no idea" was very like the "no ideas" about the dreams or the movements, but for that session at least I could get no further. In this respect the movements and the dreams were very fair instances of mutilated attempts at co-operation, and this too was something to which I had drawn his attention.

65. It may have occurred to you, as it often had to me, that I was watching a series of miniature dramatic presentations, preparations for a baby's bath or feed, or a change of nappies, or a sexual seduction. More often it would be correct to say that the presentation was a conglomeration of bits out of a number of such scenes, and it was this impression that led me finally to suppose that I was watching an ideo-motor activity, that is to say a means of expressing an idea without naming it. From this it was a short step to think of it as the kind of motor activity which Freud had described as characteristic of the supremacy of the pleasure principle (1). For, in so far as I was watching psychotic phenomena, the patient could not be acting in response to awareness of external reality; he was exhibiting the kind of motor discharge which Freud said under the supremacy of the pleasure principle "had served to unburden the mental apparatus of accretions of stimuli, and in carrying out this task had sent innervations into the interior of the body (mien expressions of affect)." It was this impression which returned to me when the patient said, "I don't expect I shall do anything today." It was a remark that could refer to the likelihood of his producing any material for interpretation or, equally, to the likelihood that I would produce any interpretations. "I ought to have rung up my mother" could mean that his failure to do so was being visited upon him by the punishment of not being able to do any analysis. It also meant that his mother would have known what to do about it—she could get associations out of him or interpretations out of me; something depended on what his mother meant to him, but on this point I was really in the dark. She had come in to the analysis as a simple working-class woman who had to go to work for the family; this view was entertained with the same degree of conviction that stamped his statements that the family were extremely wealthy. I was vouchsafed glimpses of her as a woman with such multitudinous social engagements that scant time was left her to satisfy the needs either of the patient, who was her eldest son, her eldest daughter, two years older than the patient, or the remainder of the family. She had been spoken of, if anything so inarticulate could be described as speech, as devoid of common sense or culture, though in the habit of visiting art galleries of international fame. I was left to infer that the bringing up of her children was ignorant and painstaking in the extreme. I may say that at the time of which I write I knew little more of his real mother than would be known by a person who had rid himself of his ego in the way I have described as typical of the psychotic personality. Nevertheless I had these impressions, and other which I omit, and on them I based my interpretations. The patient's responses to these interpretations were outright rejection as either quite inadmissible because wrong, or accurate but improperly arrived at in that I must have been using his mind (really his capacity for contact with reality) without his permission. It will be observed that he thereby expresses a jealous denial of my insight.

66. When the patient said, after a pause, that he knew it would be like this, I felt on fairly sure ground in assuming that it was I who was unlikely to do anything in that session and that his mother was some person or thing who could have enabled him to deal with me more satisfactorily. This impression was strengthened by the next association.

If the theories I have described are correct, then, in any given situation, the patient who is ill enough, as this one was, to have achieved certification, has two main problems to solve, one appertaining to the non-psychotic part of the personality and one to the psychotic part. With this particular patient, at this particular juncture, the psychotic personality and its problems still obscured the non-psychotic personality and its problems. Nevertheless, as I hope to show, the latter were discernible in the material. The non-psychotic personality was concerned with a neurotic problem, that is to say a problem that centred on the resolution of a conflict of ideas and emotions to which the operation of the ego had given rise. But the psychotic personality was concerned with the problem of repair of the ego, and the clue to this lay in the fear that he had lost his sight. Since it was the psychotic problem that obtruded I dealt with that, taking his last association first. I told him that these filthy things and smells were what he felt he had made me do, and that he felt he had compelled me to defecate them out, including the sight he had put in to me.

The patient jerked convulsively and I saw him cautiously scanning what seemed to be the air around him. I accordingly said that he felt surrounded by bad and smelly bits of himself including his eyes which he felt he had expelled from his anus. He replied: "I can't see." I then told him he felt he had lost his sight and his ability to talk to his mother, or to me, when he had got rid of these abilities so as to avoid pain.

67. In this last interpretation I was making use of a session, many months earlier, in which the patient complained that analysis was torture, memory torture. I showed him then that when he felt pain, as evidenced in this session by the convulsive jerks, he achieved anaesthesia by getting rid of his memory and anything that could make him realize pain.

Patient: "My head is splitting; maybe my dark glasses."

Now some five months previously I had worn dark glasses;

the fact had, as far as I could tell, produced no reaction whatever from that day to this, but that becomes less surprising if we consider that I, wearing dark glasses, was felt by him as one of the objects to which I referred when describing the fate of the expelled particles of ego. I have explained that the psychotic personality seems to have to await the occurrence of an apt event before it feels it is in possession of an ideograph suitable for use in communication with itself or with others. Reciprocally, other events, which might be supposed to have immediate significance for the non-psychotic personality, are passed by because they are felt to be significant only as ideographs serving no immediate need. In the present instance the problem created by my wearing dark glasses was obscured in the non-psychotic part of the personality because the psychotic part of the personality was dominant: and in that part of the personality the event was merely significant as an ideograph for which it had had no immediate need. When at last the fact obtruded in analysis it had the appearance, superficially, of being perhaps some kind of delayed reaction, but such a view depends on the supposition that the association of the dark glasses was an expression of neurotic conflict in the non-psychotic part of the personality. In fact it was not a delayed expression of a conflict in the non-psychotic part of the personality but, as I shall show, the mobilization of an ideograph needed by the psychotic part of the personality for an immediate repair of an ego damaged by the excessive projective identification that I have described. Such obtrusions of fact, originally passed by in silence, must then be regarded not so much as significant because their appearance is delayed, but because they are evidence of activity in the psychotic part of the personality.

Assuming then that the dark glasses here are a verbal communication of an ideograph it becomes necessary to determine the interpretation of the ideograph. I shall have to compress, almost I fear to the point of risking incomprehensibility, the evidence in my possession. The glasses contained a hint of the baby's bottle. They were two glasses, or bottles, thus resembling the breast. They were dark because frowning and angry. They were of glass to pay him out for trying to see through them when they were breasts. They were dark because he needs darkness to spy on the parents in intercourse. They were dark because he had taken the bottle not to get milk but to see what the parents did. They were dark because he had swallowed them, and not simply the milk they had contained. And they were dark because the clear good objects had been made black and smelly inside them. All these attributes must have been achieved through the operation of the non-psychotic part of the personality. Added to these characteristics were those that I have described as appertaining to them as part of the ego that has been expelled by projective identification, namely their hatred of him as part of himself he had rejected. Making use of these accretions of analytic experience, and still concentrating on the psychotic problem, that is to say, the need to repair the ego to meet the demands of the external situation, I said:

Analyst. Your sight has come back into you but splits your head; you feel it is very bad sight because of what you have done to it.

Patient (moving in pain as if protecting his back passage). Nothing.

Analyst. It seemed to be your back passage.

Patient. Moral strictures.

I told him that his sight, the dark glasses, were felt as a conscience that punished him, partly for getting rid of them to avoid pain, partly because he had used them to spy on me, and on his parents. I could not feel I had done justice to the compactness of the association.

It will be observed that I have not been able to offer any suggestions as to what might be stimulating these reactions in the patient. This is not surprising, for I am dealing with a psychotic problem, and since the psychotic problem as opposed to the non-psychotic problem is precisely related to the destruction of all the mental apparatus that brings awareness of stimuli from reality, the nature and even existence of such stimuli would not be discernible. However, the patient's next remark gave it.

Patient. The week-end; don't know if I can last it.

This is an instance of the way in which the patient felt he had repaired his capacity for contact and could therefore tell me what was going on around him. It was a phenomenon by now familiar to him and I did not interpret it. Instead I said:

Analyst. You feel that you have to be able to get on without me. But to do that you feel you need to be able to see what happens around you, and even to be able to contact me; to be able to contact me at a distance, as you do your mother when you ring her up; so you tried to get your ability to see and talk back again from me.

Patient. Brilliant interpretation. (With a sudden convulsion) O God!

Analyst. You feel you can see and understand now, but what you see is so brilliant that it causes intense pain.

Patient (clenching his fists and showing much tension and anxiety). I hate you.

Analyst. When you see, what you see—the week-end break and the things you use darkness to spy on—fills you with hate of me and admiration.

It is my belief that at this point the restoration of the ego meant that the patient was confronted with the non-psychotic problem, the resolution of neurotic conflicts. This was supported by the reactions in the following weeks, when he would display his inability to tolerate the neurotic conflicts stimulated by reality and his attempt to solve that problem by projective identification. This would be followed by attempts to use me as his ego, anxieties about his insanity, further attempts to repair his ego and return to reality and neurosis; and so the cycle would repeat itself.

68. I have described this portion of a session in detail because it can be used to illustrate a number of points without burdening the reader with a number of different examples of association and interpretation. I have regretfully had to exlude some striking and dramatic material, because to include it without including a quite overwhelming mass of description of day-to-day mundane analysis with its load of sheer incomprehensibility, error, and so forth would produce an entirely misleading picture. At the same time I do not wish to leave any doubt that the approach I am describing is one which in my opinion is producing striking results. The change that took place in this patient during the weeks when I was able to demonstrate the interplay I have just described, was of a kind that I believe any analyst would accept as worth the name of psycho-analytic improvement. The patient's demeanour softened: his expression became much less tense. At the beginnings and ends of sessions he met my eyes and did not either evade me or, what with him had been a common event, focus beyond me as if I were the surface of a mirror before which he rehearsed some inner drama, a peculiarity that had often helped me to realize that I was not a real person to him. Unfortunately these phenomena are not easy to describe and I cannot dwell on the attempt; for I wish to draw attention to an improvement which I found, and still find with other patients, both surprising and baffling. As it touches the main theme of this paper I can deal with it by returning to the theoretical discussion that I interrupted to introduce my clinical example.

69. If verbal thought is that which synthesizes and articulates impressions, and is thus essential to awareness of internal and external reality, it is to be expected that it will be subjected, on and off throughout analysis, to destructive splitting and projective identification. I described the inception of verbal thought as appertaining to the depressive position; but the depression that is proper to this phase is itself something to which the psychotic personality objects and therefore the development of verbal thought comes under attack, its inchoate elements being expelled from the personality by projective identification whenever depression occurs. In her paper to the International Congress of 1955 Segal (11) described the manner in which the psyche deals with depression; I would refer you to that description as apposite to that part of the depressive position which I here include in the discussion of the development of verbal thought. But I have said that in the even earlier phase, the paranoid-schizoid position, thought processes that should be developing are in fact being destroyed. At this stage there is no question of verbal thought but only of inchoation of primitive thought of a preverbal kind. Excessive projective identification at this early stage prevents smooth introjection and assimilation of sense impressions and so denies the personality a firm base on which the inception of pre-verbal thought can proceed. Furthermore, not only is thought attacked, as itself being a link, but the factors which make for coherence in thought itself are similarly attacked so that in the end the elements of thought, the units, as it were, of which thought is made up, cannot be articulated. The growth of verbal thought is therefore compromised both by the continuing attacks I have described as typical of the depressive position, and by the fact of the long history of attacks on thought of any kind that precedes this.

The attempt to think, which is a central part of the total process of repair of the ego, involves the use of primitive pre-verbal modes which have suffered mutilation and projective identification. This means that the expelled particles of ego, and their accretions, have to be brought back into control and therefore into the personality. Projective identification is therefore reversed and these objects are brought back by the same route as that by which they were expelled. This was expressed by a patient who said he had to use an intestine, not a brain, to think with, and emphasized the accuracy of his description by correcting me when, on a subsequent occasion, I spoke of his having taken in something by swallowing it; the intestine does not swallow, he said. In order to bring them back, these objects have to be compressed. Owing to the hostility of the rejected function of articulation, itself now an object, the objects can only be joined inappropriately, or agglomerated. I suggested in my clinical example that the dark glasses were an instance of this kind of agglomeration of bizarre objects which were the product of projective identification of the ego. Furthermore, that owing to the patient's inability to distinguish between such objects and real objects he frequently had to wait for appropriate events to provide him with the ideograph his impulse to communicate required, and that this case was a reciprocal of this, namely an instance of the storing of an event not on account of its neurotic significance but on account of its value as an ideograph. Now this means that this particular use of dark glasses is fairly advanced. For one thing the storage of such an event for use as an ideograph approximates to Freud's description of a search for data, so that they might be already familiar, if an urgent inner need should arise, as a function of attention as one of the aspects of the ego. But it also shows, albeit in this instance in a somewhat rudimentary form, a skilful agglomeration which is successful in conveying meaning. Now the surprising, and even disconcerting, improvement of which I spoke touches this point of skilful agglomeration. For I have found not only that patients resorted more and more to ordinary verbal thought, thus showing an increased capacity for it and increased consideration for the analyst as an ordinary human being, but also that they seemed to become more and more skilful at this type of agglomerated rather than articulated speech. The whole point about civilized speech is that it greatly simplifies the thinker's or speaker's task. With that tool problems can be solved because at least they can be stated, whereas without it certain questions, no matter how important, cannot even be posed. The extraordinary thing is the tour de force by which primitive modes of thought are used by the patient for the statement of themes of great complexity. And I find it significant that his ability to do this improves concurrently with more welcome advances. I say more welcome because I have not yet satisfied myself that it is right to ignore the content of an association because dealing with it would keep the analyst talking at infinitely greater length than the patient. What, for example, is the correct interpretation of the content of moral strictures? And having decided that, what is the correct procedure? For how long is one to continue the elucidation?

The particles which have to be employed share, as we have seen, the qualities of things. The patient seems to feel this as an additional obstacle to their re-entry. As these objects which are felt to have been expelled by projective identification become infinitely worse after expulsion than they were when originally expelled, the patient feels intruded upon, assaulted, and tortured by this re-entry even if willed by himself. This is shown, in the example I gave, by the convulsive movement of the patient and by his striking reaction to the "brilliant" interpretation. But this last also shows that the senses, as part of the expelled ego, also become painfully compressed on being taken back, and this is often the explanation of the extremely painful tactile, auditory, and visual hallucinations in the grip of which he seems to labour. Depression and anxiety, being subject to the same mechanism, are similarly intensified until the patient is compelled to deal with them by projective identification, as Segal described.

Conclusion

70. Experience of these theories in practice has convinced me that they have a real value and lead to improvements which even psycho-analysts may feel to deserve stern testing and scrutiny. Conversely, I do not think real progress with psychotic patients is likely to take place until due weight is given to the nature of the divergence between the psychotic and non-psychotic personality, and in particular the role of projective identification in the psychotic part of the personality as a substitute for regression in the neurotic part of the personality. The patient's destructive attacks on his ego and the substitution of projective identification for repression and introjection must be worked through. Further, I consider that this holds true for the severe neurotic, in whom I believe there is a psychotic personality concealed by neurosis as the neurotic personality is screened by psychosis in the psychotic, that has to be laid bare and dealt with.

REFERENCES

(1) Bion, W. R. (1953). "Notes on the Theory of Schizophrenia." *Int. J. Psycho-Anal.*, Vol. 35, 1954.

(2) Freud, S. "Formulations Regarding the Two Principles in Mental Functioning." Standard Ed., 12.

(3) —— (1923). *The Ego and the Id.*

(4) —— (1924). "Neurosis and Psychosis."

(5) Klein, M. (1928). "Early Stages of the Oedipus Conflict." Contributions to Psycho-Analysis, 1921–45.

(6) —— (1930). "The Importance of Symbol Formation in the Development of the Ego."

(7) —— (1946). "Notes on Some Schizoid Mechanisms." Developments in Psycho-Analysis.

(8) KLEIN, M. *Developments in Psycho-Analysis.*

(9) ROSENFELD, H. (1952). "Transference-phenomena and Transference-analysis in an Acute Catatonic Schizophrenic Patient." *Int. J. Psycho-Anal.*, Vol. 33.

(10) SEGAL, H. (1955). Paper on Symbol-formation read to the Medical Section of the British Psychological Society.

(11) —— (1956). "Depression in the Schizophrenic." *Int. J. Psycho-Anal.*, Vol. 37.

6 On Hallucination[1]

71. Descriptions of hallucinations with which I am acquainted lack the precision necessary to afford material for psycho-analytical interpretation. In this paper I describe some detailed observations of hallucination and the results that followed. I hope to persuade you that such observation of the hallucinatory processes is essential and rewarding.

The content of the paper is narrowly circumscribed and much material excluded which would be helpful to perspicuity. I must indicate two important categories of facts which suffer under this limitation. First, all the material in this paper is derived from the practical application of the theories I put forward in my paper to the British Psycho-Analytical Society on 6th October, 1955, on the Differentiation of the Psychotic from the Non-Psychotic Personalities. I am compelled to assume the reader's acquaintance with them and the acknowledgements I then made of my indebtedness to the work in this field of Melanie Klein and her co-workers. Second, I must emphasize that the clinical descriptions though disguised, come from the analysis of a patient who has been, but now is not, under certificate diagnosed as schizophrenic. Light was shed on the case by experiences with two other patients in analysis who have also been under certificate with the same diagnosis. I hope that the rest of the paper will yield the bare minimum of fact necessary for comprehension, for I shall now turn at once to the clinical descriptions.

72. The patient has arrived on time and I have asked for him to be called. As he has been with me in analysis for some years and a great deal of work has been done, I am not surprised when he appears without further ado, though such unceremonious progression has not always been the rule. As he passes into the room he glances rapidly at me; such frank scrutiny has been a development of the past six months

[1] *International Journal of Psycho-Analysis*, Vol. 39, Part 5, 1958.

and is still a novelty. While I close the door he goes to the foot of the couch, facing the head pillows and my chair, and stands, shoulders stooping, knees sagging, head inclined to the chair, motionless until I have passed him and am about to sit down. So closely do his movements seem to be geared with mine that the inception of my movements to sit appears to release a spring in him. As I lower myself into my seat he turns left about, slowly, evenly, as if something would be spilled, or perhaps fractured, were he to be betrayed into a precipitate movement. As I sit the turning movement stops as if we were both parts of the same clockwork toy. The patient, now with his back to me, is arrested at a moment when his gaze is directed to the floor near that corner of the room which would be to his right and facing him if he lay on the couch. This pause endures perhaps for a second and is closed by a shudder of his head and shoulders which is so slight and so rapid that I might suppose myself mistaken. Yet it marks the end of one phase and the start of the next; the patient seats himself on the couch preparatory to lying down.

He reclines slowly, keeping his eye on the same corner of the floor, craning his head forward now and then as he falls back on to the couch as if anxious not to become unsighted. His scrutiny, as if he feared the consequences of being detected in it, is circumspect.

He is recumbent at last; a few more surreptitious glances and he is still. Then he speaks: "I feel quite empty. Although I have eaten hardly anything, it can't be that. No, it's no use; I shan't be able to do any more today." He then relapses into silence.

So far this session differs little from many others. I hardly know when I began to notice, amongst the varying forms of opening, the features to which I have drawn attention in this account. The pattern must often have been there, though overlaid, as it seemed to me at the time, by other features that required more urgent interpretation. The gradual obtrusion, through constant repetition, of a pattern of behaviour which, when I recognized it, seemed already to be familiar, was a common experience with this patient. For the present I wish to discuss one aspect only of the features that have a bearing on hallucination.

When the patient glanced at me he was taking a part of me into him. It was taken into his eyes, as I later interpreted his thought to him, as if his eyes could suck something out of me. This was then removed from me, before I sat down, and expelled, again through his eyes, so that it was deposited in the right-hand corner of the room where he could keep it under observation while he was lying on the couch. The expulsion took a moment or two to complete. The shudder I have described was the sign that the expulsion was completed. Then, and only then, was the hallucination in being. I do not suggest that all this was revealed to me through the patient's behaviour in this series of sessions. It had emerged gradually over the years until finally it was borne in on me, and the patient in due course confirmed it, that he felt his sense organs to expel as well as to receive. This I put forward as the first step in the comprehension of hallucinatory phenomena: if the patient says he sees an object it may mean that an external object has been perceived by him or it may mean that he is ejecting an object through his eyes: if he says he hears something it may mean he is ejecting a sound—this is *not* the same as making a noise: if he says he feels something it may mean tactile sensation is being extruded, thrown off by his skin. An awareness of the double meaning that verbs of sense have for the psychotic sometimes makes it possible to detect an hallucinatory process before it betrays itself by more familiar signs.

To turn now to the content of the hallucination: what is it? First I confine my attention to the object supposedly deposited in the corner of the room: I am led to it because, judging by his glances, that is what most exercises the patient's mind. Evidently it is an hostile object: its extrusion has emptied the patient: its presence threatens him and makes him fear he will be able to make no further use of the session. The nature of his inspection of it and such meaning as lies easily accessible on the surface of his disjointed phrases tell me that much.

But in addition, I have in mind the end of the previous

day's session. The patient had been hostile and afraid that he would murder me. I was able to show him that he was splitting off painful feelings, mostly envy and revenge, of which he hoped to rid himself by forcing them into me. There the session ended. Melanie Klein has described how this mechanism produces problems for the patient by engendering fear of the analyst who now is a container of a bad part of himself. I was familiar with this sequence in this patient's analysis, so I was prepared to find that a session ending in this way would overflow into the next. And so it did; developments in the session I am describing showed I was correct to interpret his behaviour as an attempt to remove from me these bad aspects of himself before he attempted the main business of the session, the ingestion of cure.

73. Hallucinations and the fantasy of the senses as ejecting as well as receiving, point to the severity of the disorder from which the patient is suffering, but I must indicate a benign quality in the symptom which was certainly not present earlier. Splitting, evacuatory use of the senses, and hallucinations were all being employed in the service of an ambition to be cured, and may therefore be supposed to be creative activities. To contrast this experience with similar episodes earlier will help to illuminate both. First the late experience has a coherence, a degree of integration, which was quite lacking in any early session. Even the disjointed sentences yield an impression without much difficulty: the bizarre automaton-like synthesis of physical movement in which patient and analyst are geared together like clockwork toys does bring two objects together even though the relationship has been denuded of life. Finally the splitting is akin to that described by Melanie Klein as a separation of the bad breast from the good breast, of love from hate. This patient had attempted to bring objects together at least three and a half years before this. They were brought together with such violence that fission and fusion were adumbrated in terms of atomic explosions. Finally the splitting with which I have been familiar through the whole analysis has been altering its character until in the example I have given it is achieved with a degree of gentleness,

and a regard for psychic structure and function, which makes it doubtful whether an appellation that is justified by the historical development of the patient's analysis is any longer justified by the intrinsic nature of the activity. Freud used the terms splitting and dissociation indifferently ("Some Points in a Comparative Study of Hysterical and Organic Paralyses"), but it seems to me that the phenomena which I have observed in this and other severely disturbed patients are best described by the term "splitting" as it is used by Melanie Klein, leaving the term "dissociation" free to be employed where a more benign activity is being discussed. The original splitting processes evinced by this patient were violent, intended to produce minute fragmentation and deliberately aimed at effecting separations which run directly counter to any natural lines of demarcation between one part of the psyche, or one function of the psyche, and another. Dissociation on the other hand appears to be gentler and to have respect for natural lines of demarcation between whole objects and indeed to follow those lines of demarcation to effect the separation; the patient who dissociates is capable of depression. Dissociation also appears to me to betray dependence on the pre-existence of elementary verbal thought, as indeed Freud's statement that "it is the common popular idea of the organs and of the body in general that is at work in the hysterical paralyses" would seem to indicate. Where I wish to stress the developmental aspect of the activity in the history of the patient's analysis I shall continue to use the term splitting: where I wish to speak of a benign process related to the non-psychotic part of the personality I shall speak of dissociation.

I hope it is now clear that I am speaking of a psychotic patient who has achieved a stage of development in which creative impulses are discernible and can even be detected as motives in mental mechanisms which at the beginning of his analysis appeared to be wholly subservient to wishes to destroy.

I did not on this occasion give the patient the explanations I have given here, for, as I have said, he was by this time familiar with the fact that he was not sure whether any given sensation was a sign that something was being taken in by him or a sign that something had been, or was being, expelled by him. It may give an idea of some of the difficulties of interpretation if I recount an episode from one of the early sessions in which the nature of the hallucinatory experience was becoming more evident. I had drawn the patient's attention to the fact that when he said, with every evidence of persecutory anxiety, "Tears are coming to my eyes", he meant that these tears were coming into his eyes from outside and were going to blind him. He thereupon sat up and stared at the opposite wall with much the same demeanour and bearing that he exhibited in the course of the expulsion of an object into the right-hand corner of the room that I have been describing. When, as it appeared to me, the evacuation was complete, he said, "A man told me it was good to be depressed." I was pretty sure that I was the man and that that is what he had heard me say, but I felt I lacked any supporting evidence that would make an interpretation on those lines relevant, and said, "You are seeing that man in front of you now, I think." He replied, "It's all gone dark. I can't see. I'm shut in." This response may appear to be as puzzling as it did to me, until I realized that the patient felt, when psychotic mechanisms were in the forefront of his mental activity, that the same mechanisms and modes of thought were being employed by me. Thanks to familiarity with this fact, I was able to realize that the patient thought I must have seen the man who was visible to him. As I have explained elsewhere, the bizarre objects with which the psychotic part of the personality feels itself to be surrounded when projective identification is over-active, are always compounded of a variety of elements of which one is a part of the personality of the patient himself. If, therefore, I had seen the man, a part of the patient's personality which was mingled with this object, had been sucked into me through my eyes. It will be realized that I am describing in some detail the clinical manifestation of the confusional states which have been described by Melanie Klein and confirmed by Herbert Rosenfeld. I therefore told him that he felt that a part of himself had been greedily swallowed up by my eyes which had taken in not only the man he saw, but a bit of him too.

To return to the session which I am using as the main source of my clinical material for this paper: I resume my description from the point where I had interpreted the hallucinatory activity as an attempt to deal with the dangerous parts of his personality. I have said that the patient relapsed into silence after his disjointed sentences. While I gave my interpretation he made jerky convulsive movements which were confined mostly to the upper part of his body. Each syllable that I uttered seemed to be felt by him as a stabbing thrust from me. I pointed this out and said that he felt a very bad thing was being violently intruded into him, partly by me, who he thought was trying to get rid of the object he had left inside me, and partly by himself in spite of the precaution he had taken by hardly eating anything. His greed remained, though he no longer wished to be greedy, because it was now felt to be independent of any control by himself.

I did not explain my reference to greed because I assumed that the patient was by this time familiar, through work which we had previously done, with the fact that he often used his eyes as organs of ingestion so that his greed could be satisfied, though his object strove to preserve itself by denying him physical contact. In this instance my assumption proved correct, but in fact I have often found that such assumptions, which if successful enable me to preserve the interpretation from being overburdened with detail, have proved to be beyond the patient's grasp until his capacity for integration is developed.

The convulsive movements stopped and he said, "I have painted a picture." His subsequent silence meant that the material for my next interpretation was already in my possession.

74. The lineaments of the picture that he has painted must be sought in the totality of material of which my interpretation so far has illuminated only one aspect, namely that which I adumbrated as centring on the bad object which he had withdrawn from me and immediately deposited in the right-hand corner of the room. My task, therefore, was to consider all the events of the session up to this point, as if it were a palimpsest in which I must detect another pattern whose outline was confused with that which I had already revealed in my interpretation. Before I passed on to a consideration of this pattern, I interpreted to the patient an aspect of this situation to which I draw your attention. It is that the patient is playing a dominant role, and expressing, with an unusual degree of urgency and force, a belief in his capacity to communicate matters, which he feels to be worth while, to a person whom he thinks likely to be receptive of them. But, I said, I was in addition a part of the picture which he had painted when he made himself and myself into two automata in a reciprocal but lifeless relationship. He replied, "The wireless next door kept me awake last night."

I knew that strong persecutory feelings were associated by him with all electrical apparatus, and I said he felt attacked by the electricity which he felt was like the life and sex which he had removed from the two objects which he had pushed out of himself when he painted his picture. He said, "Quite right" and then remarked that he did not know what would happen after the session, which in fact ended at this point.

This session, like some others, which achieved a similar degree of integration, was called by the patient a "good" session, and to some extent this may be accepted as a gratifying confirmation of a judgement I was myself disposed to make. But I had noticed that such sessions were followed with great consistency by "bad" sessions, that is, sessions in which the patient seemed to return to an apparently unco-operative state of mind and produced material which I, as likely as not, found it almost impossible to interpret. His preoccupation with what would occur after the session was partly due to his own realization of this. He disliked the prospect of losing what he now recognized as an agreeable state of mind, namely, that which accompanied his awareness of co-operation. Work on this had revealed a number of contributory causes, such as: hatred and envy of analyst or patient, or the collaboration of both, for a successful creative achievement; a method of expiating guilt at benefiting; or expiation of guilt at having engaged in what, being a friendly co-operation, was to the patient a sexual act. In the session I have described this last point might be expected to apply with peculiar force and cogency, especially in view of the implication in my interpretation that a sexual bond, though denied, was to be supposed to exist.

In fact the session following did have many of the features of the so-called bad session, though my reason for reporting it is for the light it shed on our problems and not because of the lack of it. I find the description of such a session very difficult, because it is not possible to make notes, however soon after a session, of long passages of verbalization whose meaning, if any, eluded me. I am prepared to vouch for a reasonable degree of accuracy in my report of behaviour that I was able to interpret.

The patient came in, gave me a swift glance, waited till I reached my chair, and then lay down without further ado. He said tonelessly: "I don't know how much I shall be able to do today. As a matter of fact I got on quite well yesterday." At this point I felt his attention began to wander and he faltered in his speech. This kind of opening was quite familiar as a prelude to the bad session. He went on: "I am definitely anxious. Slightly. Still I suppose that does not matter." Rapidly becoming more incoherent, he continued, "I asked for some coffee. She seemed upset. It may have been my voice. but it was definitely good coffee too. I don't know why I shouldn't like it. When I passed the mews I thought the walls bulged outwards. I went back later but it was all right." There was more that I cannot attempt to reconstruct. He continued to speak, hesitatingly, with minor pauses, for some five or more minutes. On the whole the sample I have given is fairly representative of the material, except that the reference to the coffee and the mews had by this stage in the analysis a good many associations for the patient and me, but the subsequent material had no associative value that I knew of, whatever it might mean to him.

75. As I have said, this kind of behaviour was familiar to me. It had been the rule in the early stages of analysis and was common after "good" sessions, but I must say more of this now to clarify the nature of the problem confronting me in this session. Although it is not apparent in the account I have given, this patient was capable of coherent verbal expression. Within the last year he had on one occasion shown me that he was capable of making a psycho-analytic review of some emotional experience he had been through with good insight into his state of mind and good understanding of the analytic work done in the previous years of analysis. It had been in response to an interpretation which he seemed to take as a slight on his understanding, but it had shown that he had in fact learned much and could use it. Nothing could be in greater contrast than the state of mind revealed in that outburst and the state of mind which he usually presented and with which he was confronting me in the session I now describe. It seemed as if all the interpretations I had ever given needed to be given all over again, but it was equally obvious, that these interpretations would tell him nothing new. Indeed, his response to the interpretation I did give him showed that my suspicion was correct. I pointed out that he was showing me how "much" he could do, but without regard to the quality. He replied that he had placed his gramophone on the seat, which was his way of indicating that my interpretation combined the characteristics of a recording with which he was familiar and a defecation. I had reason, very shortly after that, to suppose that this response was far more than a mere criticism.

I was unwilling to repeat interpretations that I felt reasonably sure he could make for himself, but nevertheless there were borderline instances where I felt repetition was called for. The effect of these interpretations was not encouraging to further efforts of the same kind. I felt I had exhausted my supply of explanations and was more exercised with the possible causes of the patient's return to a pattern of behaviour which seemed to disprove the efficacy of any analytical approach to his problems. Something must have happened, but what? I drew his attention to the fact that he was having what he often called a "bad" session and that there must be a reason. He seemed to accept the fact but offered no explanation, nor could I detect any in his material. The one reason that did not occur to me but which, in the light of later events, might have led me to some illumination of the material, was the possibility that he had had a dream.

This patient had begun occasionally to report dreams to me. It was a comparatively recent development, some three or four months only, but in the absence of associations I had not felt able to make much headway beyond a few somewhat obvious suggestions such as that he felt it was something important to tell me or that he felt I would be the kind of person who understood them.

76. I cannot say now what it was in the session that first made me realize that the patient was hallucinated. It may have been that he was so manipulating the analysis and myself that I felt I was no longer an independent object, but was being treated by him as an hallucination. My suspicion was that when he said he had placed his gramophone on the seat he was denying me life and independent existence in the analytic chair and treating my interpretations as auditory hallucinations. I did not immediately interpret this, but said that it appeared that he was reactivating a state of mind which, we must assume, it had now become important to him to preserve as a good object. His response to this was to move his head and eyes as if my words were visible objects which were passing over his head to become impacted on the opposite wall. This behaviour was familiar from an early stage, and indeed I had seen it in other patients. Rodriguez reports similar behaviour in a psychotic child. On previous occasions I had interpreted his behaviour to mean that he saw my words as things and was following them with his eyes. He had shown relief, almost amounting to amusement, and he appeared to agree that my words were seen as evacuated objects like bits of faeces. It had seemed to me then that the hallucination had a reassuring quality in that my interpretations, felt as persecutory objects, were seen to be passing harmlessly overhead. I said that he was again seeing objects passing overhead and reminded him of the previous occasion. This time he became anxious and said, "I feel quite empty. Better to close my eyes." He remained silent and very anxious and then said, somewhat apologetically I thought. "I have to use my ears. I seem to hear things all wrong." This association brought it to my mind that he was not observing a direct relationship between myself and the opposite wall, as I had supposed to be the case on earlier occasions. My interpretation was being taken in by his ears, but in a way which he felt to be "all wrong"—that is to say, cruelly and destructively. If so, the interpretations were being taken in and transformed by his ears and ejected by his eyes. This seemed so extraordinary that it was a moment or two before the explanation flashed upon me. I gave it in the following interpretation: "You", I said to him, "are feeling that your ears are chewing up and destroying all that I say to you. You are so anxious to get rid of it that you at once expel the pieces out of your eyes." I reminded him that when he had wished greedily to take something in, he did so through his eyes, because his eyes could reach a long way to things he could not possibly touch with his mouth. I went on, "You are now using your eyes for the opposite reason, that is to say, to throw these broken up bits of interpretation as far away from yourself as you possibly can." The patient seemed extremely frightened, yet there was relief in his voice when he agreed. I drew his attention to his fear. He replied that he felt too weak to go on, "I am fading out." I suggested that he was afraid of me because he felt he was destroying me as well as my interpretations and also afraid because he could not get enough interpretations to cure him. This interpretation enabled him to go on with his associations. They were similar to those at the beginning of the session, yet there was a difference. He said that he had seen a painting in D——. It had a penis in it. He complained that he had ruined a painting by making it pretty instead of ugly. He then said, "All sounds turn into things I see around me." I interpreted that he was again turning my interpretations into sounds and then evacuating them through his eyes, so that he now saw them as objects surrounding him. He replied, "Then everything around me is made by me. This is megalomania." After a pause he said, "I like your interpretation very much." In parenthesis, I must add that from this time onward I was able to recognize how very common it was for the patient, when he received an interpretation which for some reason was unwelcome, to give evidence of becoming hallucinated. He would strain forward on the couch as if looking at something in a far corner of the room. It became clear that these were frequent repetitions of the mechanism I have been describing. I shall suggest later some of the implications of this substitute for denial.

77. At this point his associations became less coherent. Unfortunately, I cannot report this material with any accuracy for reasons which I hope will be apparent. The associations seemed to consist of parts of sentences, disjointed references to what I assumed to be actual events, and a certain amount of material which had a meaning for me because it had appeared in other sessions. For an appreciable time my attention dwelt on this parade of associations to the exclusion of a peculiar accompaniment of running commentary on how he was feeling. As this obtruded, I became aware of a pattern which went like this: association, association, association, "definitely a bit anxious", association, association, "yes, slightly depressed", associations, "a bit anxious now", and so on. His behaviour was striking, but the session came to an end without my being able to formulate any clear idea of what was going on. I said that we did not know why all his analytic intuition and understanding had disappeared. He said "Yes" commiseratingly, and if one word can be made to express "and I think that your intuition must have gone too", then his "Yes" did so on this occasion.

He started the next session in the matter-of-fact tone that he employed on the rare occasions when he spoke rationally and coherently. "I had a peculiar dream", he said, "it was a day or two ago." His voice became depressed during the course of this short communication, and by the end of it I felt that all trace of the matter-of-fact tone had gone. "You were in it", he added. It was clear that I was not going to hear any more about this dream, at any rate for the present, and that there were going to be no associations to it. I was not unduly disturbed by this because I had already been led to some conclusions about the nature of psychotic dreams. I had noticed that much work was needed before a psychotic patient reported a dream at all, and that when he did so he seemed to feel that he had said all that was necessary in reporting the fact that he had dreamt. I felt that I was expected to say something. I was not clear why the patient called his experience a dream, and in what way he distinguished it from other experiences which, though variously described by him to me, seemed to be hallucinations. I came to the conclusion that the patient meant that it was something that happened to him at night, when he was in bed, and probably when he was asleep. I felt that the "dreams" shared so many characteristics of the hallucination that it was possible that actual experiences of hallucination in the consulting room might serve to throw light on the psychotic dream. It is a short step from what I have already said about hallucinations to suppose that when a psychotic patient speaks of having a dream, he thinks that his perceptual apparatus is engaged in expelling something and that the dream is an evacuation from his mind strictly analogous to an evacuation from his bowels. A patient cannot report a dream until much analytic work has been done, and he cannot have done that analytic work without feeling that if he, as it were, passes a dream, he must at some time have taken that dream in. In short, to the psychotic a dream is an evacuation of material that has been taken in during waking hours. Much development must take place before the psychotic dream becomes sufficiently coherent to be communicable at all. Before that, I doubt whether its connexion with objects perceived is ever made. After that, I think it always is. Bearing this in mind, an approach to understanding the patient's dream becomes simpler. There is still a point: why does the patient say he had a *peculiar* dream? I hoped the session would throw light on this. In the meantime I said that this dream, together with the "good" session, had been the cause which we had not found for reactivation of the state of mind in the "bad" session. He replied, "I was mad." He had described these states of mind, when hallucinations, splitting, projective identification and confusion were dominant as "mad" or "insane" before. I made no observation on this, but used the term "mad" myself whenever it served as a rapid method of referring to this complex state. I did so now. "You seem to feel", I said, "that you are mad when you are denying my interpretations by taking them in and getting rid of them at once. You must have felt that they have something to do with the peculiar dream. Why are you moving like that?"

My question was prompted by a series of convulsive twitchings of his chest. He said he did not know. "My thoughts go too quickly."

78. Whenever the patient had exhibited this kind of action, at least in the latter stages of his analysis, I had been reminded of Freud's description of motor activity, before the establishment of the reality principle, as not directed to alteration of the environment but to an unburdening of "the mental apparatus of accretions of stimuli." I said it was his way of showing his feelings. "Like smiling", he replied. His movements then ceased, and he began a series of associations which seemed to have the same characteristics as those I described as occurring at the latter end of the previous session. Still wondering why the dream should be regarded by the patient as peculiar, I listened to his disjointed associations with the running commentary to me of "anxious", "slightly anxious", and "depressed". After some time I thought I discerned a pattern. It was as if his stream of associations were by way of being a prolonged evacuation; some were merely disjointed phrases, others far more articulate. Although I could not be sure, I thought that his report of anxiety was associated with the more fragmented material, his report of depression with such parts as tended to be articulated wholes. I therefore said, "Your dream has frightened and upset you because when I came into it you felt I was a real person whom your mind had swallowed up and was losing while you slept. It made you think that during your analysis you must have been greedily destroying a real person and not just a thing." He at once began to talk quite rationally about a visit that he planned to make to see his brother. I drew his attention to the change in his behaviour since I had made the interpretation about his dream. He replied, "What dream?" And then, as if to cover up his bewilderment, said, "Oh yes: I think I must have forgotten", but in fact I did not have the impression he had recalled the dream. A little later he said he felt he he had made some progress, but felt very depressed, he did not know why. Work during the next fortnight convinced me that my suspicions about his dream, and the interpretations I based on them, were substantially correct. I was confirmed in my impression that the appearance of whole objects in dreams, and elsewhere, is at one and the same moment a sign of progress and a forerunner of depression which may reach a dangerous intensity if its source is not elucidated. The "peculiarity" of the dream to the psychotic is not its irrationality, incoherence, and fragmentation, but its revelation of objects which are felt by the patient to be whole objects and therefore fit and proper reason for the powerful feelings of guilt and depression which Melanie Klein has associated with the onset of the depressive position. Their presence is felt to be evidence that real and valued objects have been destroyed. The immediate oscillation to fragmentation, however, does not, as I have shown in my account of the stream of associations with a running commentary on the patient's feelings, afford any true relief, because it merely substitutes persecutory anxiety for the dread depression.

There are two dangerous features in the situation I am describing. H. Rosenfeld has pointed out how a patient who brings fragments together to make a whole object can be so disturbed by the cohesion of the fragments that an immediate explosive fragmentation follows. I supported his findings in my paper "Some Notes on the Theory of Schizophrenia", and would now bring forward the events I then described for comparison with this less explosive yet dangerous alternation I am now describing. The danger here lies in the possibility of suicide, on the one hand, or, on the other, a return to the paranoid-schizoid position that is characterized by a secondary fragmentation which is imposed on the already severe primary fragmentation that Melanie Klein has described as characteristic of the paranoid-schizoid position. It seems as if the patient, regressing from the depressive position, turns with increased hatred and anxiety against the fragments that have shown their power to coalesce and splits them with great thoroughness; as a result we have a danger of a fragmentation so minute that reparation of the ego becomes impossible and the prospects of the patient correspondingly hopeless.

I regard this phase of advance to, and retreat from, the depressive position as critical, not least because the danger of suicide is liable to obscure the significance of the retreat to the paranoid-schizoid position, and in particular the fact that secondary splitting is an inherent factor in the retreat and one which, if not detected and interpreted, is liable not merely to jeopardize promising developments of the analysis, but also to reverse the whole process and usher in a deterioration from which no recovery is possible.

79. Understanding of the material demands reference to certain collateral phenomena. During the period when this work that I have been describing was done, the patient was complaining that he could not distinguish between what was real and what was unreal, that he did not know whether something was an hallucination or not. In my paper on the Differentiation of the Psychotic from the Non-psychotic Personalities, I described one of the consequences of the excessive use of projective identification as a state in which the patient felt he was surrounded by bizarre objects compounded partly of real objects and partly of fragments of the personality, and in particular those aspects of the personality listed putatively by Freud as being in the course of normal development called into being under the dominance of the reality principle. Amongst these aspects of the personality was the patient's capacity for judgement. The patient's complaint that he could not distinguish the real from the unreal was one of the consequences of this expulsion from his psyche, by the mechanism of projective identification, of his capacity for judgement. From the theory I then propounded it would be natural to suppose that amongst these bizarre objects it should be possible to trace something analogous to a capacity for judgement. From my experience I am persuaded that these particular bizarre objects are to be found in what are ordinarily described as the patient's "delusions". In his paper on Constructions in Analysis

(1937), Freud suggests that delusions may be the "equivalents of the constructions which we build up in the course of an analytic treatment—attempts at explanation and cure. . . .", though he points out that under the conditions of a psychosis they are bound to be ineffectual. It appeared to me, during this period of the analysis, that the patient's delusions had this aspect, and that some of his delusions were attempts at employing bizarre objects in the service of therapeutic intuition. If so, it may afford a definition of the relationship between delusion and hallucination.

80. I shall close this description with two comments which are, I think, significant. The first concerns the nature of the hallucinatory experiences which I have been describing. They seem to approximate more closely to what Freud described as hysterical hallucinations than the psychotic hallucinations which were exclusively in evidence in the earlier phases of the analysis. I would say that the development of this difference was directly related to an increase in the patient's capacity to tolerate depression. A differentiation of two types of hallucination, hysterical and psychotic, could be referred to a difference in content. The hysterical hallucination contains whole objects and is associated with depression; the psychotic hallucination contains elements analogous to part-objects. Both types are to be found in the psychotic patient. I shall conclude this paper by drawing attention to certain features of it on which I have done work that cannot be communicated at this juncture. *First*, the patient's fear of committing murder owes much of its intensity to his belief that he has already been guilty of it. The reasons for this belief emerge in associations of which I have given one example in the charade-like episode, when he was coupled with myself, so that both appeared as lifeless automatons. It will be remembered that he is there guilty of removing a life which then becomes a persecutory object, the radio that embodies electricity, sex, and life itself. The episode shows how guilt is evaded by resort to persecution by the life that has been destroyed. *Second*, the fear of making a murderous attack is intensified by the patient's awareness of the extent to which he is dominated by a state of mind and feeling appropriate to that phase of development which Freud described as under the sway of the pleasure principle. Freud suggested that in that phase the patient's actions are not directed towards a change in the environment, but are intended rather to unburden the psychic apparatus of accretions of stimuli and therefore correspond to muscular movements of the kind involved in changes of mien and expression. Let us suppose that in this state of mind the patient feels an impulse to express feelings of love towards a girl whom he regards as a prospective mate: furthermore, that he feels obstructed in this aim by the presence of feelings of impotence together with feelings of hatred and envy towards the sexual parents who are thought by him to possess, and to deny him the use of, the potent breast or penis that makes the possessor potent in the expression of love. In this state he is dominated by feelings of impotence, envy, and a hatred which is further strengthened by a sense of frustration and inability to tolerate the frustration. Over all is the sense of obstructed love. At once the need becomes imperative, in the service of expression of the feelings of love for his object, to disburden his psyche of destructive hate and envy. The lack of any impulse to alter the environment, together with the wish for speed that is associated with the inability to tolerate frustration, contribute to forcing a resort to muscular action of the kind characteristic of the phase of dominance by the pleasure principle; for experience has shown the patient that action of that kind achieves its purpose far more swiftly than action directed to alteration of the environment. The unburdening of the psyche by hallucination, that is by the use of the sensory apparatus in reverse, is reinforced by muscular action which may best be understood as being an extremely complex analogue of a scowl; the musculature does not simply change the expression to one of murderous hate but gives effect to an actual murderous assault. The resultant act must, therefore, be understood as an ideo-motor activity and is felt by the patient to appertain to that class of phenomena that I have described as creating bizarre objects. He does not feel he has altered his environment, but he does feel that he is now free to love his object without any conflicting feelings of impotence, hatred or envy. Such relief is short-lived. This description is an approximation to the state of mind of which the patient is dreadfully aware in the non-psychotic part of his personality. It contributes to his fear of any progress that might lead him to form loving attachments which would give rise to desires to express his love. and from that to intolerance of the frustration preserved by the existence of his destructive impulses, and from that to being overwhelmed by the psychotic part of his personality in which only he can find mechanisms that hold promise of instantaneous solution of the problems presented by the existence of unwanted emotions. The danger which the patient fears is, therefore, one he has good reason to fear. It can be stated in analytic terms as follows: He wishes to love. Feeling incapable of frustration he resorts to a murderous assault, or a token assault, as a method of disburdening his psyche of the unwanted emotions. The assault is but the outward expression of an explosive projective identification by virtue of which his murderous hatred, together with bits of his personality, is scattered far and wide into the real objects, members of society included, by which he is surrounded. He now feels free to be loving, but is surrounded by bizarre objects each compounded of real people and things, destructive hatred, and murderous conscience. The picture is further complicated because, although it is true to say the patient feels free to love, at least in intention, the violence of the explosion leaves him denuded also of his feelings of love.

81. From all that I have said it may now be seen that in the event of the patient making an actual assault a complex situation has arisen, and that this situation can for simplicity of description be resolved into the following elements. First, the patient's resort to an omnipotent fantasy as a means towards loving his object. Second, an external manifestation, which in fact, though not by the patient's intent, affects the environment and incidentally gives the analyst his material on which he bases his interpretations. Third, in extreme cases, a reaction of society to the external manifestation, which is itself complex and compounded, amongst other elements, of psychotic reactions typical of unconscious collusion in receiving the projective identifications of one of its members. Fourth, the resort to projective identification as a substitute for repression, to which I referred on the 6th October, 1955, implies a weakness of a capacity for denial, and this is shown by the resort to destructive attacks upon the perceptual apparatus, and by the use of perceptual apparatus. of which he is in fact unable to rid himself, for expulsion of unwanted stimuli as they are received. The attempt to rid himself of his perceptual system leads to compensatory hypertrophy of sense impressions, e.g. Lord Adrian's distant perception. Fifth, the danger that, in the course of the analysis, the patient will become incurable through an unanalysed retreat from the depressive position to the paranoid-schizoid position, in the course of which secondary splitting will be imposed upon the primary splitting intrinsic to his original experience of the paranoid-schizoid position; the danger lies in the minute fragmentation which results from this renewal of splitting and the impossibility thereafter of effecting any reparation. Sixth, the relation of depression to the appearance of what the patient feels to be whole objects in material expelled from his personality. Seventh, the analyst's need to appreciate that the presence of hallucinations is much more frequent than is realized, and depends upon the fact that, the senses being two-way, an object may be to the patient an excretion, or, as we should say, an hallucination, rather than something existing independently of himself. A striking example of this is presented when the patient sees double with one eye. Eighth, the relation of over-action of expulsion to megalomania.

82. This summary list may serve to indicate the possibilities for further research which are opened up by attempting that close and detailed observation of hallucinations for which I hope I have made out a case.

7 On Arrogance[1]

83. In this paper I propose to deal with the appearance, in the material of a certain class of patient, of references to curiosity, arrogance and stupidity which are so dispersed and separated from each other that their relatedness may escape detection. I shall suggest that their appearance should be taken by the analyst as evidence that he is dealing with a psychological disaster. The meaning with which I wish to invest the term "arrogance" may be indicated by supposing that in the personality where life instincts predominate, pride becomes self-respect, where death instincts predominate, pride becomes arrogance.

Their separation from each other and the lack of evidence of any relatedness is evidence that a disaster has occurred. To make clear the connection between these references, I shall rehearse the Oedipus myth from a point of view which makes the sexual crime a peripheral element of a story in which the central crime is the arrogance of Oedipus in vowing to lay bare the truth at no matter what cost.

84. This shift of emphasis brings the following elements into the centre of the story: the sphinx, who asks a riddle and destroys herself when it is answered, the blind Teiresias, who possesses knowledge and deplores the resolve of the king to search for it, the oracle that provokes the search which the prophet deplores, and again the king who, his search concluded, suffers blindness and exile. This is the story of which the elements are discernible amongst the ruins of the psyche, to which the scattered references to curiosity, arrogance, and stupidity have pointed the way.

I said that these references are significant in a certain class of patient; the class to which I refer is one in which psychotic mechanisms are active and have to be analytically uncovered before a stable adjustment can be achieved. In practice,

[1] Paper read before the 20th Congress of the International Psycho-Analytical Association, Paris, July-August 1957.

analysis of such a patient may seem to follow the patterns with which we are familiar in the treatment of the neuroses, but with the important difference that improvement in the patient's condition does not appear to be commensurate with the analytic work that is done. To recapitulate, the analyst who is treating an apparently neurotic patient must regard a negative therapeutic response together with the appearance of scattered, unrelated references to curiosity, arrogance and stupidity as evidence that he is in the presence of a psychological catastrophe with which he will have to deal.

85. It may be supposed that an approach to the problem is provided by the emergence in the analysis of one of these references, and this is in fact the case. It is important that reference to any of these three qualities should be treated by the analyst as a significant event demanding investigation and provoking more than usually stubborn resistances. Unfortunately the problem is complicated by a fact which must be already evident, and that is that the analytic procedure itself is precisely a manifestation of the curosity which is felt to be an intrinsic component of the disaster. As a consequence, the very act of analysing the patient makes the analyst an accessory in precipitating regression and turning the analysis itself into a piece of acting out. From the point of view of successful analysis, this is a development that should be avoided. Yet I have not been able to see how this can be done. The alternative course is to accept the acting out and regression as inevitable, and if possible to turn it to good account. This, I believe, can be done, but it involves detailed interpretation of events that are taking place in the session. These events are active displays of the mechanisms of splitting, projective identification, and the related subsidiary phenomena of confusional states, depersonalization and hallucination, which have been described by Melanie Klein, Segal, and Rosenfeld as part of the analysis of psychotic patients.

86. In this phase of the analysis, the transference is peculiar in that, in addition to the features to which I have drawn attention in previous papers, it is to the analyst as analyst. Features of this are his appearance, and that of the patient in so far as he is identified with the analyst as, by turns, blind, stupid, suicidal, curious, and arrogant. I shall have more to say later about the qualities of arrogance. I must emphasize that at this stage the patient would appear to have no problems other than the existence of the analyst himself. Furthermore that the spectacle presented is one, to borrow Freud's analogy, similar to that of the archaeologist who discovers in his field-work the evidences, not so much of a primitive civilization, as of a primitive catastrophe. In analytic terms that hope must be that the investigations which are being carried out will issue in the reconstitution of the ego. This aim is, however, obscured because this analytic procedure has become an acting out of destructive attacks launched against the ego, wherever it is discerned. That is to say, the ego whether it appears manifest in the patient or the analyst. These attacks closely resemble the description given by Melanie Klein of the infant's fantasied attacks on the breast.

87. If we now turn to consider what there is in reality that makes it so hateful to the patient that he must destroy the ego which brings him into contact with it, it would be natural to suppose that it is the sexually orientated Oedipus situation, and indeed I have found much to substantiate this view. When reconstitution of the ego has proceeded sufficiently to bring the Oedipus situation into sight, it is quite common to find that it precipitates further attacks on the ego. But there is evidence that some other element is playing an important part in provoking destructive attacks on the ego and its consequent disintegration. The key to this lies in the references to arrogance which I promised to explore further.

Briefly, it appears that overwhelming emotions are associated with the assumption by the patient or analyst of the qualities required to pursue the truth, and in particular a capacity to tolerate the stresses associated with the introjection of another person's projective identifications. Put into other terms, the implicit aim of psycho-analysis to pursue the truth at no matter what cost is felt to be synonymous with a claim to a capacity for containing the discarded, split-off aspects of other personalities while retaining a balanced outlook. This would appear to be the immediate signal for outbreaks of envy and hatred.

88. I propose now to devote the remainder of this paper to description of the clinical aspect of the material which I have so far approached theoretically. The patient in question did not at any time behave in a way which in my view would warrant a diagnosis of psychosis; he had, however, displayed the features I have mentioned, namely, scattered references to curiosity, arrogance, and stupidity together with what I felt was an inadequate therapeutic response. At the period with which I deal, the significance of these features had become clear and I had been able to give him some insight into their relatedness and the increasing frequency with which they appeared in the forefront of his material. He described his behaviour in the sessions as mad or insane, and he showed anxiety at his inability to behave in a way which his experience of analysis had shown him to be helpful in furthering analytic progress. For my part I was impressed by the fact that for several sessions at a time he seemed to be devoid of the insight and judgement which I knew from previous experience that he possessed. Furthermore, the material was almost entirely of the kind with which I was familiar in the analysis of psychotic patients. That is to say, projective identification was extremely active, and the patient's states of confusion and depersonalization easy to detect and frequently in evidence. For a matter of some months sessions were taken up entirely with psychotic mechanisms to an extent which made me wonder how it was that the patient was apparently continuing his extra-analytic life without, as far as I knew, any material change for the worse.

89. I shall not describe this stage further, as it does not differ from previous accounts of work with the psychotic patient. I wish to concentrate on that aspect of the analysis which relates to a particular form of internal object.

In its simplest form this material appeared in sessions when the patient's associations lacked coherence and consisted of "sentences" which were remarkably deficient in one or the other aspect of the grammar of conversational English. Thus, a significant object might be mentioned, but there would be no pronoun or verb, or a significant verbal form would appear such as "going skating", but there would be no mention of who was supposed to be doing this or where, and so on in an apparently inexhaustible number of variations. The establishment of an analytically potent relationship by means of verbal communication thus seemed to be impossible. Analyst and patient together formed a frustrated couple. This in itself was not new, and on one occasion, during a relatively lucid session, the patient himself observed that the method of communication was so mutilated that creative work was impossible, and he despaired of the possibility that any cure would come about. He was already quite familiar with the sexual anxiety inherent in such conduct, so it seemed reasonable to suppose that some progress would follow, and it was the more surprising that this did not in fact happen; the anxiety of the patient increased. I was eventually forced to assume, on theoretical grounds, that progress had taken place and that there was a change in his behaviour which I was failing to observe. With this assumption in mind I attempted to cast about for some revealing clue which would indicate what this change might be. In the meantime the sessions continued much as before. I remained at a loss until one day, in a lucid moment, the patient said he wondered that I could stand it. This gave me a clue: at least I now knew that there was something I was able to stand which he apparently could not. He realized already that he felt he was being obstructed in his aim to establish a creative contact with me, and that this obstructive force was sometimes in him, sometimes in me, and sometimes occupied an unknown location. Furthermore, the obstruction was effected by some means other than mutilation or verbal communications. The patient had already made it clear that the obstructing forces or object was out of his control.

90. The next step forward occurred when the patient said that I was the obstructing force, and that my outstanding characteristic was "that I could not stand it". I now worked on the assumption that the persecuting object that could not permit any creative relationship was one that "could not stand it", but I was still not clear what "it" was. It was tempting to assume that "it" was any creative relationship which was made intolerable to the persecuting object through envy and hate of the creative couple. Unfortunately this did not lead any further because it was an aspect of the material which had already been made clear without producing any advance. The problem of what "it" was still, therefore, awaited solution.

Before I discuss this problem further, I must mention a feature of the material which had led up to this point, because it contributes to an understanding of the next step. During the whole of this period which I have been describing, references to curosity, arrogance, and stupidity became more frequent and more obviously related to each other. The stupidity was purposeful, and arrogance, not always called by that name, was sometimes an accusation, sometimes a temptation, and sometimes a crime. The cumulative effect of these references was to persuade me that their relatedness depended upon their association with the obstructive object. Curiosity and stupidity waxed or waned together; that is to say, if curiosity increased, so did the stupidity. I therefore felt some gain in knowledge of the character of the obstructive force. What it was that the object could not stand became clearer in some sessions where it appeared that in so far as I, as analyst, was insisting on verbal communication as a method of making the patient's problems explicit, I was felt to be directly attacking the patient's methods of communication. From this it became clear that when I was identified with the obstructive force, what I could not stand was the patient's methods of communication. In this phase my employment of verbal communication was felt by the patient to be a mutilating attack on *his* methods of communication. From this point onwards, it was only a matter of time to demonstrate that the patient's link with me was his ability to employ the mechanism of projective identification. That is to say, his relationship with me and his ability to profit by the association lay in the opportunity to split off parts of his psyche and project them into me.

On this depended a variety of procedures which were felt

to ensure emotionally rewarding experiences such as, to mention two, the ability to put bad feelings in me and leave them there long enough for them to be modified by their sojourn in my psyche, and the ability to put good parts of himself into me, thereby feeling that he was dealing with an ideal object as a result. Associated with these experiences was a sense of being in contact with me, which I am inclined to believe is a primitive form of communication that provides a foundation on which, ultimately, verbal communication depends. From his feelings about me when I was identified with the obstructive object, I was able to deduce that the obstructive object was curious about him, but could not stand being the receptacle for parts of his personality and accordingly made destructive and mutilating attacks, largely through varieties of stupidity, upon his capacity for projective identification. I, therefore, concluded that the catastrophe stemmed from the mutilating attacks made upon this extremely primitive species of link between the patient and analyst.

Conclusion

91. In some patients the denial to the patient of a normal employment of projective identification precipitates a disaster through the destruction of an important link. Inherent in this disaster is the establishment of a primitive superego which denies the use of projective identification. The clue to this disaster is provided by the emergence of widely separated references to curiosity, arrogance, and stupidity.

8 Attacks on Linking[1]

92. In previous papers (3) I have had occasion, in talking of the psychotic part of the personality, to speak of the destructive attacks which the patient makes on anything which is felt to have the function of linking one object with another. It is my intention in this paper to show the significance of this form of destructive attack in the production of some symptoms met with in borderline psychosis.

The prototype for all the links of which I wish to speak is the primitive breast or penis. The paper presupposes familiarity with Melanie Klein's descriptions of the infant's fantasies of sadistic attacks upon the breast (6), of the infant's splitting of its objects, of projective identification, which is the name she gives to the mechanism by which parts of the personality are split off and projected into external objects, and finally her views on early stages of Oedipus complex (5). I shall discuss phantasied attacks on the breast as the prototype of all attacks on objects that serve as a link and projective identification as the mechanism employed by the psyche to dispose of the ego fragments produced by its destructiveness.

I shall first describe clinical manifestations in an order dictated not by the chronology of their appearance in the consulting room, but by the need for making the exposition of my thesis as clear as I can. I shall follow this by material selected to demonstrate the order which these mechanisms assume when their relationship to each other is determined by the dynamics of the analytic situation. I shall conclude with theoretical observations on the material presented. The examples are drawn from the analysis of two patients and are taken from an advanced stage of their analyses. To preserve anonymity I shall not distinguish between the patients and shall introduce distortions of fact which I hope do not impair the accuracy of the analytic description.

[1] *International Journal of Psycho-Analysis*, Vol. 40, Parts 5–6, 1959.

Observation of the patient's disposition to attack the link between two objects is simplified because the analyst has to establish a link with the patient and does this by verbal communication and his equipment of psycho-analytical experience. Upon this the creative relationship depends and therefore we should be able to see attacks being made upon it.

I am not concerned with typical resistance to interpretations, but with expanding references which I made in my paper on "The Differentiation of the Psychotic from the Non-psychotic Part of the Personality" (3) to the destructive attacks on verbal thought itself.

Clinical Examples

93. I shall now describe occasions which afforded me an opportunity to give the patient an interpretation, which at that point he could understand, of conduct designed to destroy whatever it was that linked two objects together.

These are the examples:

(i) I had reason to give the patient an interpretation making explicit his feelings of affection and his expression of them to his mother for her ability to cope with a refractory child. The patient attempted to express his agreement with me, but although he needed to say only a few words his expression of them was interrupted by a very pronounced stammer which had the effect of spreading out his remark over a period of as much as a minute and a half. The actual sounds emitted bore resemblance to gasping for breath; gaspings were interspersed with gurgling sounds as if he were immersed in water. I drew his attention to these sounds and he agreed that they were peculiar and himself suggested the descriptions I have just given.

(ii) The patient complained that he could not sleep. Showing signs of fear, he said, "It can't go on like this". Disjointed remarks gave the impression that he felt superficially that some catastrophe would occur, perhaps akin to insanity, if he could not get more sleep. Referring to material in the previous session I suggested that he feared he would dream if he were to sleep. He denied this and said he could not think because he was wet. I reminded him of his use of the term "wet" as an expression of contempt for somebody he regarded as feeble and sentimental. He disagreed and indicated that the state to which he referred was the exact opposite. From what I knew of this patient I felt that his correction at this point was valid and that somehow the wetness referred to an expression of hatred and envy such as he associated with urinary attacks on an object. I therefore said that in addition to the superficial fear which he had expressed he was afraid of sleep because for him it was the same thing as the oozing away of his mind itself. Further associations showed that he felt that good interpretations from me were so consistently and minutely split up by him that they became mental urine which then seeped uncontrollably away. Sleep was therefore inseparable from unconsciousness, which was itself identical with a state of mindlessness which could not be repaired. He said, "I am dry now". I replied that he felt he was awake and capable of thought, but that this good state was only precariously maintained.

(iii) In this session the patient had produced material stimulated by the preceding week-end break. His awareness of such external stimuli had become demonstrable at a comparatively recent stage of the analysis. Previously it was a matter for conjecture how much he was capable of appreciating reality. I knew that he had contact with reality because he came for analysis by himself, but that fact could hardly be deduced from his behaviour in the sessions. When I interpreted some associations as evidence that he felt he had been and still was witnessing an intercourse between two people, he reacted as if he had received a violent blow. I was not then able to say just where he had experienced the assault and even in retrospect I have no clear impression. It would seem logical to suppose that the shock had been administered by my interpretation and that therefore the blow came from without, but my impression is that he felt it as delivered from within; the patient often experienced what he described as a stabbing attack from inside. He sat up and stared intently into space. I said that he seemed to be seeing something. He replied that he could not see what he saw. I was able from previous experience to interpret that he felt he was "seeing" an invisible object and subsequent experience convinced me that in the two patients on whose analysis I am depending for material for this paper, events occurred in which the patient experienced invisible-visual hallucinations. I shall give my reasons later for supposing that in this and the previous example similar mechanisms were at work.

(iv) In the first twenty minutes of the session the patient made three isolated remarks which had no significance for me. He then said that it seemed that a girl he had met was understanding. This was followed at once by a violent, convulsive movement which he affected to ignore. It appeared to be identical with the kind of stabbing attack I mentioned in the last example. I tried to draw his attention to the movement, but he ignored my intervention as he ignored the attack. He then said that the room was filled with a blue haze. A little later he remarked that the haze had gone, but said he was depressed. I interpreted that he felt understood by me. This was an agreeable experience, but the pleasant feeling of being understood had been instantly destroyed and ejected. I reminded him that we had recently witnessed his use of the word "blue" as a compact description of vituperative sexual conversation. If my interpretation was correct, and subsequent events suggested that it was, it meant that the experience of being understood had been split up, converted into particles of sexual abuse and ejected. Up to this point I felt that the interpretation approximated closely to his experience. Later interpretations, that the disappearance of the haze was due to reintrojection and conversion into depression, seemed to have less reality for the patient, although later events were compatible with its being correct.

(v) The session, like the one in my last example, began with three or four statements of fact such as that it was hot, that his train was crowded, and that it was Wednesday; this occupied thirty minutes. An impression that he was trying to retain contact with reality was confirmed when he followed up by saying that he feared a breakdown. A little later he said I would not understand him. I interpreted that he felt I was bad and would not take in what he wanted to put into me. I interpreted in these terms deliberately because he had shown in the previous session that he felt that my interpretations were an attempt to eject feelings that he wished to deposit in me. His response to my interpretation was to say that he felt there were two probability clouds in the room. I interpreted that he was trying to get rid of the feeling that my badness was a fact. I said it meant that he needed to know whether I was really bad or whether I was some bad thing which had come from inside him. Although the point was not at the moment of central significance I thought the patient was attempting to decide whether he was hallucinated or not. This recurrent anxiety in his analysis was associated with his fear that envy and hatred of a capacity for understanding was leading him to take in a good, understanding object to destroy and eject it—a procedure which had often led to persecution by the destroyed and ejected object. Whether my refusal to understand was a reality or hallucination was important only because it determined what painful experiences were to be expected next.

(vi) Half the session passed in silence; the patient then announced that a piece of iron had fallen on the floor. Thereafter he made a series of convulsive movements in silence as if he felt he was being physically assaulted from within. I said he could not establish contact with me because of his fear of what was going on inside him. He confirmed this by saying that he felt he was being murdered. He did not know what he would do without the analysis as it made him better. I said that he felt so envious of himself and of me for being able to work together to make him feel better that he took the pair of us into him as a dead piece of iron and a dead floor that came together not to give him life but to murder him. He became very anxious and said he could not go on. I said that he felt he could not go on because he was either dead, or alive and so envious that he had to stop good analysis. There was a marked decrease of anxiety, but the remainder of the session was taken up by isolated statements of fact which again seemed to be an attempt to preserve contact with external reality as a method of denial of his phantasies.

Features Common to the Above Illustrations

94. These episodes have been chosen by me because the dominant theme in each was the destructive attack on a link. In the first the attack was expressed in a stammer which was designed to prevent the patient from using language as a bond between him and me. In the second sleep was felt by him to be identical with projective identification that proceeded unaffected by any possible attempt at control by him. Sleep for him meant that his mind, minutely fragmented, flowed out in an attacking stream of particles.

The examples I give here throw light on schizophrenic dreaming. The psychotic patient appears to have no dreams, or at least not to report any, until comparatively late in the analysis. My impression now is that this apparently dreamless period is a phenomenon analogous to the invisible-visual hallucination. That is to say, that the dreams consist of material so minutely fragmented that they are devoid of any visual component. When dreams are experienced which the patient can report because visual objects have been experienced by him in the course of the dream, he seems to regard these objects as bearing much the same relationship to the invisible objects of the previous phase as faeces seem to him to bear to urine. The objects appearing in experiences which we call dreams are regarded by the patient as solid and are, as such, contrasted with the contents of the dreams which were a continuum of minute, invisible fragments.

At the time of the session the main theme was not an attack on the link but the consequences of such an attack, previously made, in leaving him bereft of a state of mind necessary for the establishment of a satisfying relationship between him and his bed. Though it did not appear in the session I report, uncontrollable projective identification, which was what sleep meant to him, was thought to be a destructive attack on the state of mind of the coupling parents. There was therefore a double anxiety; one arising from his fear that he was being rendered mindless, the other from his fear that he was unable to control his hostile attacks, his mind providing the ammunition, on the state of mind that was the link between the parental pair. Sleep and sleeplessness were alike unacceptable.

In the third example in which I described visual hallucinations of invisible objects, we witness one form in which the actual attack on the sexual pair is delivered. My interpretation as far as I could judge, was felt by him as if it were his own visual sense of a parental intercourse; this visual impression is minutely fragmented and ejected at once in particles so minute that they are the invisible components of a continuum. The total procedure has served the purpose of forestalling an experience of feelings of envy for the parental state of mind by the instantaneous expression of envy in a destructive act. I shall have more to say of this implicit hatred of emotion and the need to avoid awareness of it.

In my fourth example, the report of the understanding girl and the haze, my understanding and his agreeable state of mind, have been felt as a link between us which could give rise to a creative act. The link had been regarded with hate and transformed into a hostile and destructive sexuality rendering the patient-analyst couple sterile.

In my fifth example, of the two probability clouds, a capacity for understanding is the link which is being attacked but the interest lies in the fact that the object making the destructive attacks is alien to the patient. Furthermore, the destroyer is making an attack on projective identification which is felt by the patient to be a method of communication. In so far as my supposed attack on his methods of communication is felt as possibly secondary to his envious attacks on me, he does not dissociate himself from feelings of guilt and responsibility. A further point is the appearance of judgement, which Freud regards as an essential feature of the dominance of the reality principle, among the ejected parts of the patient's personality. The fact that there were two probability clouds remained unexplained at the time, but in subsequent sessions I had material which led me to suppose that what had originally been an attempt to separate good from bad survived in the existence of two objects, but they were now similar in that each was a mixture of good and bad. Taking into consideration material from later sessions,

I can draw conclusions which were not possible at the time; his capacity for judgement, which had been split up and destroyed with the rest of his ego and then ejected, was felt by him to be similar to other bizarre objects of the kind which I have described in my paper on "The Differentiation of the Psychotic from the Non-psychotic parts of the Personality". These ejected particles were feared because of the treatment he had accorded them. He felt that the alienated judgement—the probability clouds—indicated that I was probably bad. His suspicion that the probability clouds were persecutory and hostile led him to doubt the value of the guidance they afforded him. They might supply him with a correct assessment or a deliberately false one, such as that a fact was an hallucination or vice versa; or would give rise to what, from a psychiatric point of view, we would call delusions. The probability clouds themselves had some qualities of a primitive breast and were felt to be enigmatic and intimidating.

In my sixth illustration, the report that a piece of iron had fallen on the floor, I had no occasion for interpreting an aspect of the material with which the patient had by this time become familiar. (I should perhaps say that experience had taught me that there were times when I assumed the patient's familiarity with some aspect of a situation with which we were dealing, only to discover that, in spite of the work that had been done upon it, he had forgotten it.) The familiar point that I did not interpret, but which is significant for the understanding of this episode, is that the patient's envy of the parental couple had been evaded by his substitution of himself and myself for the parents. The evasion failed, for the envy and hatred were now directed against him and me. The couple engaged in a creative act are felt to be sharing an enviable, emotional experience; he, being identified also with the excluded party, has a painful, emotional experience as well. On many occasions the patient, partly through experiences of the kind which I describe in this episode, and partly for reasons on which I shall enlarge later, had a hatred of emotion, and therefore, by a short extension, of life itself. This hatred contributes to the murderous attack on that which links the pair, on the pair itself and on the object generated by the pair. In the episode I am describing, the patient is suffering the consequences of his early attacks on the state of mind that forms the link between the creative pair and his identification with both the hateful and creative states of mind.

In this and the preceding illustration there are elements that suggest the formation of a hostile persecutory object, or agglomeration of objects, which expresses its hostility in a manner which is of great importance in producing the predominance of psychotic mechanisms in a patient; the characteristics with which I have already invested the agglomeration of persecutory objects have the quality of a primitive, and even murderous, superego.

Curiosity, Arrogance and Stupidity

95. In the paper I presented at the International Congress of 1957 (4) I suggested that Freud's analogy of an archaeological investigation with a psycho-analysis was helpful if it were considered that we were exposing evidence not so much of a primitive civilization as of a primitive disaster. The value of the analogy is lessened because in the analysis we are confronted not so much with a static situation that permits leisurely study, but with a catastrophe that remains at one and the same moment actively vital and yet incapable of resolution into quiescence. This lack of progress in any direction must be attributed in part to the destruction of a capacity for curiosity and the consequent inability to learn, but before I go into this I must say something about a matter that plays hardly any part in the illustrations I have given.

Attacks on the link originate in what Melanie Klein calls the paranoid-schizoid phase. This period is dominated by part-object relationships (8). If it is borne in mind that the patient has a part-object relationship with himself as well as with objects not himself, it contributes to the understanding of phrases such as "it seems" which are commonly employed by the deeply disturbed patient on occasions when a less disturbed patient might say "I think" or "I believe". When he says "it seems" he is often referring to a feeling—an "it seems" feeling—which is a part of his psyche and yet is not observed as part of a whole object. The conception of the part-object as analogous to an anatomical structure, encouraged by the patient's employment of concrete images as units of thought, is misleading because the part-object relationship is not with the anatomical structures only but with function, not with anatomy but with physiology, not with the breast but with feeding, poisoning, loving, hating. This contributes to the impression of a disaster that is dynamic and not static. The problem that has to be solved on this early, yet superficial level, must be stated in adult terms by the question, "What is something?" and not the question "Why is something?" because "why" has, through guilt, been split off. Problems, the solution of which depends upon an awareness of causation, cannot therefore be stated, let alone solved. This produces a situation in which the patient appears to have no problems except those posed by the existence of analyst and patient. His preoccupation is with what is this or that function, of which he is aware though unable to grasp the totality of which the function is a part. It follows that there is never any question why the patient or the analyst is there, or why something is said or done or felt, nor can there be any question of attempting to alter the causes of some state of mind. . . . Since "what?" can never be answered without "how?" or "why?" further difficulties arise. I shall leave this on one side to consider the mechanisms employed by the infant to solve the problem "what?" when it is felt in relation to a part-object relationship with a function.

Denial of Normal Degrees of Projective Identification

96. I employ the term "link" because I wish to discuss the patient's relationship with a function rather than with the object that subserves a function; my concern is not only with the breast, or penis, or verbal thought, but with their function of providing the link between two objects.

In her *Notes on Some Schizoid Mechanisms* (7) Melanie Klein speaks of the importance of an excessive employment of splitting and projective identification in the production of a very disturbed personality. She also speaks of "the introjection of the good object, first of all the mother's breast" as a "precondition for normal development". I shall suppose that there is a normal degree of projective identification, without defining the limits within which normality lies, and that associated with introjective identification this is the foundation on which normal development rests.

This impression derives partly from a feature in a patient's analysis which was difficult to interpret because it did not appear to be sufficiently obtrusive at any moment for an interpretation to be supported by convincing evidence. Throughout the analysis the patient resorted to projective identification with a persistence suggesting it was a mechanism of which he had never been able sufficiently to avail himself; the analysis afforded him an opportunity for the exercise of a mechanism of which he had been cheated. I did not have to rely on this impression alone. There were sessions which led me to suppose that the patient felt there was some object that denied him the use of projective identification. In the illustrations I have given, particularly in the first, the stammer, and the fourth, the understanding girl and the blue haze, there are elements which indicate that the patient felt that parts of his personality that he wished to repose in me were refused entry by me, but there had been associations prior to this which led me to this view.

When the patient strove to rid himself of fears of death which were felt to be too powerful for his personality to contain he split off his fears and put them into me, the idea apparently being that if they were allowed to repose there long enough they would undergo modification by my psyche and could then be safely reintrojected. On the occasion I have in mind the patient had felt, probably for reasons similar to those I give in my fifth illustration, the probability clouds, that I evacuated them so quickly that the feelings were not modified, but had become more painful.

Associations from a period in the analysis earlier than that from which these illustrations have been drawn showed an increasing intensity of emotions in the patient. This originated in what he felt was my refusal to accept parts of his personality. Consequently he strove to force them into me with increased desperation and violence. His behaviour, isolated from the context of the analysis, might have appeared to be an expression of primary aggression. The more violent his phantasies of projective identification, the more frightened he became of me. There were sessions in which such behaviour expressed unprovoked aggression, but I quote this series because it shows the patient in a different light, his violence a reaction to what he felt was my hostile defensiveness. The analytic situation built up in my mind a sense of witnessing an extremely early scene. I felt that the patient had experienced in infancy a mother who dutifully responded to the infant's emotional displays. The dutiful response had in it an element of impatient "I don't know what's the matter with the child." My deduction was that in order to understand what the child wanted the mother should have treated the infant's cry as more than a demand for her presence. From the infant's point of view she should have taken into her, and thus experienced, the fear that the child was dying. It was this fear that the child could not contain. He strove to split it off together with the part of the personality in which it lay and project it into the mother. An understanding mother is able to experience the feeling of dread, that this baby was striving to deal with by projective identification, and yet retain a balanced outlook. This patient had had to deal with a mother who could not tolerate experiencing such feelings and reacted either by denying them ingress, or alternatively by becoming a prey to the anxiety which resulted from introjection of the infant's feelings. The latter reaction must, I think, have been rare: denial was dominant.

To some this reconstruction will appear to be unduly fanciful; to me it does not seem forced and is the reply to any who may object that too much stress is placed on the transference to the exclusion of a proper elucidation of early memories.

In the analysis a complex situation may be observed. The patient feels he is being allowed an opportunity of which he had hitherto been cheated; the poignancy of his deprivation is thereby rendered the more acute and so are the feelings of resentment at the deprivation. Gratitude for the opportunity coexists with hostility to the analyst as the person who will not understand and refuses the patient the use of the only method of communication by which he feels he can make himself understood. Thus the link between patient and analyst, or infant and breast, is the mechanism of projective identification. The destructive attacks upon this link originate in a source external to the patient or infant, namely the analyst or breast. The result is excessive projective identification by the patient and a deterioration of his developmental processes.

I do not put forward this experience as the cause of the patient's disturbance; that finds its main source in the inborn disposition of the infant as I described it in my paper on "The Differentiation of the Psychotic from the Non-psychotic Part of the Personality" (3). I regard it as a central feature of the environmental factor in the production of the psychotic personality.

Before I discuss this consequence for the patient's development, I must refer to the inborn characteristics and the part that they play in producing attacks by the infant on all that links him to the breast, namely, primary aggression and envy. The seriousness of these attacks is enhanced if the mother displays the kind of unreceptiveness which I have described, and is diminished, but not abolished, if the mother can introject the infant's feelings and remain balanced (9); the seriousness remains because the psychotic infant is overwhelmed with hatred and envy of the mother's ability to retain a comfortable state of mind although experiencing the infant's feelings. This was clearly brought out by a patient who insisted that I must go through it with him, but was filled with hate when he felt I was able to do so without a breakdown. Here we have another aspect of destructive attacks upon the link, the link being the capacity of the analyst to introject the patient's projective identifications. Attacks on the link, therefore, are synonymous with attacks on the analyst's, and originally the mother's, peace of mind. The capacity to introject is transformed by the patient's envy and hate into greed devouring the patient's psyche; similarly, peace of mind becomes hostile indifference. At this point analytic problems arise through the patient's employment (to destroy the peace of mind that is so much envied) of acting out, delinquent acts and threats of suicide.

Consequences

97. To review the main features so far: the origin of the disturbance is twofold. On the one hand there is the patient's inborn, disposition to excessive destructiveness, hatred, and envy: on the other the environment which, at its worst, denies to the patient the use of the mechanisms of splitting and projective identification. On some occasions the destructive attacks on the link between patient and environment, or between different aspects of the patient's personality, have their origin in the patient; on others, in the mother, although in the latter instance and in psychotic patients, it can never be in the mother alone. The disturbances commence with life itself. The problem that confronts the patient is: What are the objects of which he is aware? These objects, whether internal or external, are in fact part-objects and predominantly, though not exclusively, what we should call functions and not morphological structures. This is obscured because the patient's thinking is conducted by means of concrete objects and therefore tends to produce, in the sophisticated mind of the analyst, an impression that the patient's concern is with the nature of the concrete object. The nature of the functions which excite the patient's curiosity he explores by projective identification. His own feelings, too powerful to be contained within his personality, are amongst these functions. Projective identification makes it possible for him to investigate his own feelings in a personality powerful enough to contain them. Denial of the use of this mechanism, either by the refusal of the mother to serve as a repository for the infant's feelings, or by the hatred and envy of the patient who cannot allow the mother to exercise this function, leads to a destruction of the link between infant and breast and consequently to a severe disorder of the impulse to be curious on which all learning depends. The way is therefore prepared for a severe arrest of development. Furthermore, thanks to a denial of the main method open to the infant for dealing with his too powerful emotions, the conduct of emotional life, in any case a severe problem, becomes intolerable. Feelings of hatred are thereupon directed against all emotions including hate itself, and against external reality which stimulates them. It is a short step from hatred of the emotions to hatred of life itself. As I said in my paper on "The Differentiation of the Psychotic from the Non-psychotic Part of the Personality" (3), this hatred results in a resort to projective identification of all the perceptual apparatus including the embryonic thought which forms a link between sense impressions and consciousness. The tendency to excessive projective identification when death instincts predominate is thus reinforced.

Superego

98. The early development of the superego is effected by this kind of mental functioning in a way I must now describe. As I have said, the link between infant and breast depends upon projective identification and a capacity to introject projective identifications. Failure to introject makes the external object appear intrinsically hostile to curiosity and to the method, namely projective identification, by which the infant seeks to satisfy it. Should the breast be felt as fundamentally understanding, it has been transformed by the infant's envy and hate into an object whose devouring greed has as its aim the introjection of the infant's projective identifications in order to destroy them. This can show in the patient's belief that the analyst strives, by understanding the patient, to drive him insane. The result is an object which, when installed in the patient, exercises the function of a severe and ego-destructive superego. This description is not accurate applied to any object in the paranoid-schizoid position because it supposes a whole-object. The threat that such a whole-object impends contributes to the inability, described by Melanie Klein and others (11), of the psychotic patient to face the depressive position and the developments attendant on it. In the paranoid-schizoid phase the bizarre objects composed partially of elements of a persecutory super-ego which I described in my paper on "The Differentiation of the Psychotic from the Non-psychotic Part of the Personality" are predominant.

Arrested Development

The disturbance of the impulse of curosity on which all learning depends, and the denial of the mechanism by which it seeks expression, makes normal development impossible. Another feature obtrudes if the course of the analysis is favourable; problems which in sophisticated language are posed by the question "Why?" cannot be formulated. The patient appears to have no appreciation of causation and will complain of painful states of mind while persisting in courses of action calculated to produce them. Therefore when the appropriate material presents itself the patient must be shown that he has no interest in why he feels as he does. Elucidation of the limited scope of his curiosity issues in the development of a wider range and an incipient preoccupation with causes. This leads to some modification of conduct which otherwise prolongs his distress.

Conclusions

99. The main conclusions of this paper relate to that state of mind in which the patient's psyche contains an internal object which is opposed to, and destructive of, all links whatsoever from the most primitive (which I have suggested is a normal degree of projective identification) to the most sophisticated forms of verbal communication and the arts.

In this state of mind emotion is hated; it is felt to be too powerful to be contained by the immature psyche, it is felt to link objects and it gives reality to objects which are not self and therefore inimical to primary narcissism.

The internal object which in its origin was an external breast that refused to introject, harbour, and so modify the baneful force of emotion, is felt, paradoxically, to intensify, relative to the strength of the ego, the emotions against which it initiates the attacks. These attacks on the linking function of emotion lead to an overprominence in the psychotic part of the personality of links which appear to be logical, almost mathematical, but never emotionally reasonable. Consequently the links surviving are perverse, cruel, and sterile.

The external object which is internalized, its nature, and the effect when so established on the methods of communication within the psyche and with the environment, are left for further elaboration later.

REFERENCES

(1) BION, W. R. (1954). "Notes on the Theory of Schizophrenia." *Int. J. Psycho-Anal.*, Vol. 35, Part 2.

(2) —— (1956). "Development of Schizophrenic Thought." *Int. J. Psycho-Anal.*, Vol. 37.

(3) —— (1957). "The Differentiation of the Psychotic from the Non-psychotic Part of the Personality." *Int. J. Psycho-Anal.*, Vol. 38, Parts 3–4.

(4) —— (1957). "On Arrogance." Int. Psycho-An. Congress, 1957.

(5) KLEIN, M. (1928). *Early Stages of the Oedipus Conflict.*

(6) —— (1934). "A Contribution to the Psychogenesis of Manic-Depressive States." 13th Int. Psycho-An. Congress, 1934.

(7) —— (1946). Notes on some Schizoid Mechanisms.

(8) KLEIN, M. (1948). "The Theory of Anxiety and Guilt." *Int. J. Psycho-Anal.*, Vol. 29.

(9) —— (1957). *Envy and Gratitude*, Chap. II. (Tavistock Publications, 1957.)

(10) ROSENFELD, H. (1952). "Notes on the Supergo Conflict in an Acute Schizophrenic Patient." *Int. J. Psycho-Anal.*, Vol. 33.

(11) SEGAL, H. (1950). "Some Aspects of the Analysis of a Schizophrenic." *Int. J. Psycho-Anal.*, Vol. 31, Part 4.

(12) —— (1956). "Depression in the Schizophrenic." *Int. J. Psycho-Anal.*, Vol. 37, Parts 4–5.

(13) —— (1957). "Notes on Symbol Formation." *Int. J. Psycho-Anal.*, Vol. 38, Part 6.

(Received 15 December, 1958)

9 A Theory of Thinking[1]

100. In this paper I am primarily concerned to present a theoretical system. Its resemblance to a philosophical theory depends on the fact that philsophers have concerned themselves with the same subject matter; it differs from philosophical theory in that it is intended, like all psycho-analytical theories, for use. It is devised with the intention that practising psycho-analysts should restate the hypotheses of which it is composed in terms of empirically verifiable data.

In this respect it bears the same relationship to similar statements of philosophy as the statements of applied mathematics bear to pure mathematics.

The derived hypotheses that are intended to admit of empirical test, and to a lesser extent the theoretical system itself, bear the same relationship to the observed facts in a psycho-analysis, as statements of applied mathematics, say about a mathematical circle, bear to a statement about a circle drawn upon paper.

This theoretical system is intended to be applicable in a significant number of cases; psycho-analysts should therefore experience realizations that approximate to the Theory.

I attach no diagnostic importance to the Theory though I think it may be applicable whenever a disorder of thought is believed to exist. Its diagnostic significance will depend upon the pattern formed by the constant conjunction of a number of theories of which this theory would be one.

It may help to explain the Theory if I discuss the background of emotional experience from which the Theory has been abstracted: I shall do this in general terms without attempting scientific rigour.

101. It is convenient to regard thinking as dependent on the successful outcome of two main mental developments. The first is the development of thoughts. They require an

[1] *International Journal of Psycho-Analysis*, Vol. 43, Parts 4–5, 1962.

apparatus to cope with them. The second development therefore, is of this apparatus that I shall provisionally call thinking. I repeat—thinking has to be called into existence to cope with thoughts.

It will be noted that this differs from any theory of thought as a product of thinking, in that thinking is a development forced on the psyche by the pressure of thoughts and not the other way round. Psychopathological developments may be associated with either phase or both, that is they may be related to a breakdown in the development of thoughts, or a breakdown in the development of the apparatus for "thinking" or dealing with thoughts, or both.

"Thoughts" may be classified, according to the nature of their developmental history, as pre-conceptions, conceptions or thoughts, and finally concepts; concepts are named and therefore fixed conceptions or thoughts. The conception is initiated by the conjunction of a pre-conception with a realization. The pre-conception may be regarded as the analogue in psycho-analysis of Kant's concept of "empty thoughts". Psycho-analytically the theory that the infant has an inborn disposition corresponding to an expectation of a breast may be used to supply a model. When the pre-conception is brought into contact with a realization that approximates to it, the mental outcome is a conception. Put in another way, the pre-conception (the inborn expectation of a breast, the a priori knowledge of a breast, the "empty thought") when the infant is brought into contact with the breast itself, mates with awareness of the realization and is synchronous with the development of a conception. This model will serve for the theory that every junction of a pre-conception with its realization produces a conception. Conceptions therefore will be expected to be constantly conjoined with an emotional experience of satisfaction.

I shall limit the term "thought" to the mating of a pre-conception with a frustration. The model I propose is that of an infant whose expectation of a breast is mated with a realization of no breast available for satisfaction. This mating is experienced as a no-breast, or "absent" breast inside. The next step depends on the infant's capacity for frustration: in particular it depends on whether the decision is to evade frustration or to modify it.

If the capacity for toleration of frustration is sufficient the "no-breast" inside becomes a thought and an apparatus for "thinking" it develops. This initiates the state, described by Freud in his Two Principles of Mental Functioning, in which dominance by the reality principle is synchronous with the development of an ability to think and so to bridge the gulf of frustration between the moment when a want is felt and the moment when action appropriate to satisfying the want culminates in its satisfaction. A capacity for tolerating frustration thus enables the psyche to develop thought as a means by which the frustration that is tolerated is itself made more tolerable.

If the capacity for toleration of frustration is inadequate, the bad internal "no-breast", that a personality capable of maturity ultimately recognizes as a thought, confronts the psyche with the need to decide between evasion of frustration or of its modification.

Incapacity for tolerating frustration tips the scale in the direction of evasion of frustration. The result is a significant departure from the events that Freud describes as characteristic of thought in the phase of dominance of the reality principle. What should be a thought, a product of the juxtaposition of pre-conception and negative realization, becomes a bad object, indistinguishable from a thing-in-itself, fit only for evacuation. Consequently the development of an apparatus for thinking is disturbed and instead there takes place a hypertrophic development of the apparatus of projective identification. The model I propose for this development is a psyche that operates on the principle that evacuation of a bad breast is synonymous with obtaining sub-stenance from a good breast. The end result is that all thoughts are treated as if they were indistinguishable from bad internal objects; the appropriate machinery is felt to be, not an apparatus for thinking the thoughts, but an apparatus for ridding the psyche of accumulations of bad internal objects. The crux lies in the decision between modification or evasion of frustration.

102. Mathematical elements, namely straight lines, points, circles and something corresponding to what later becomes known by the names of numbers, derive from realizations of two-ness as in breast and infant, two eyes, two feet and so on.

If intolerance of frustration is not too great modification becomes the governing aim. Development of mathematical elements, or mathematical objects as Aristotle calls them, is analogous to the development of conceptions.

If intolerance of frustration is dominant, steps are taken to evade perception of the realization by destructive attacks. In so far as pre-conception and realization are mated mathematical conceptions are formed but they are treated as if indistinguishable from things-in-themselves and are evacuated at high speed as missiles to annihilate space. In so far as space and time are perceived as identical with a bad object that is destroyed, that is to say a no-breast, the realization that should be mated with the pre-conception is not available to complete the conditions necessary for the formation of a conception. The dominance of projective identification confuses the distinction between the self and the external object. This contributes to the absence of any perception of two-ness since such an awareness depends on the recognition of a distinction between subject and object.

The relationship with time was graphically brought home to me by a patient, who said over and over again that he was wasting time—and continued to waste it. The patient's aim is to destroy time by wasting it. The consequences are illustrated in the description in Alice in Wonderland of the Mad Hatter's tea-party—it is always four o'clock.

Inability to tolerate frustration can obstruct the development of thoughts and a capacity to think, though a capacity to think would diminish the sense of frustration intrinsic to appreciation of the gap between a wish and its fulfilment. Conceptions, that is to say the outcome of a mating between a pre-conception and its realization, repeat in a more complex form the history of pre-conception. A conception does not necessarily meet a realization that approximates sufficiently closely to satisfy. If frustration can be tolerated the mating of conception and realizations whether negative or positive initiates procedures necessary to learning by experience. If intolerance of frustration is not so great as to activate the mechanisms of evasion and yet is too great to bear dominance of the reality principle, the personality develops omnipotence as a substitute for the mating of the pre-conception, or conception, with the negative realization. This involves the assumption of omniscience as a substitute for learning from experience by aid of thoughts and thinking. There is therefore no psychic activity to discriminate between true and false. Omniscience substitutes for the discrimination between true and false a dictatorial affirmation that one thing is morally right and the other wrong. The assumption of omniscience that denies reality ensures that the morality thus engendered is a function of psychosis. Discrimination between true and false is a function of the non-psychotic part of the personality and its factors. There is thus potentially a conflict between assertion of truth and assertion of moral ascendancy. The extremism of the one infects the other.

103. Some pre-conceptions relate to expectations of the self. The pre-conceptual apparatus is adequate to realizations that fall in the narrow range of circumstances suitable for the survival of the infant. One circumstance that affects survival is the personality of the infant himself. Ordinarily the personality of the infant, like other elements in the environment, is managed by the mother. If mother and child are adjusted to each other projective identification plays a role in the management through the operation of a rudimentary and fragile reality sense; usually an omnipotent phantasy, it operates realistically. This, I am inclined to believe, is its normal condition. When Melanie Klein speaks of "excessive" projective identification I think the term "excessive" should be understood to apply not to the frequency only with which projective identification is employed but to excess of belief in omnipotence. As a realistic activity it shows itself as behaviour reasonably calculated to arouse in the mother feelings of which the infant wishes to be rid. If the infant feels it is dying it can arouse fears that it is dying in the mother. A well-balanced mother can accept these and respond therapeutically: that is to say in a manner that makes the infant feel it is receiving its frightened personality back again but in a form that it can tolerate—the fears are manageable by the infant personality. If the mother cannot tolerate these projections the infant is reduced to continued projective identification carried out with increasing force and frequency. The increased force seems to denude the projection of its penumbra of meaning. Reintrojection is effected with similar force and frequency. Deducing the patient's feelings from his behaviour in the consulting room and using the deductions to form a model, the infant of my model does not behave in a way that I ordinarily expect of an adult who is thinking. It behaves as if it felt that an internal object has been built up that has the characteristics of a greedy vagina-like "breast" that strips of its goodness all that the infant receives or gives leaving only degenerate objects. This internal object starves its host of all understanding that is made available. In analysis such a patient seems unable to gain from his environment and therefore from his analyst. The consequences for the development of a capacity for thinking are serious; I shall describe only one, namely precocious development of consciousness.

By consciousness I mean in this context what Freud described as a "sense-organ for the perception of psychic qualities."

104. I have described previously (at a Scientific Meeting of the British Psycho-Analytical Society) the use of a concept of alpha-function as a working tool in the analysis of disturbances of thought. It seemed convenient to suppose an alpha-function to convert sense data into alpha-elements and thus provide the psyche with the material for dream thoughts and hence the capacity to wake up or go to sleep, to be conscious or unconscious. According to this theory consciousness depends on alpha-function and it is a logical necessity to suppose that such a function exists if we are to assume that the self is able to be conscious of itself in the sense of knowing itself from experience of itself. Yet the failure to establish, between infant and mother, a relationship in which normal projective identification is possible precludes the development of an alpha-function and therefore of a differentiation of elements into conscious and unconscious.

The difficulty is avoided by restricting the term "consciousness" to the meaning conferred on it by Freud's definition. Using the term "consciousness" in this restricted sense it is possible to suppose that this consciousness produces "sense-data" of the self but that there is no alpha-function to convert them into alpha-elements and therefore permit of a capacity for being conscious or unconscious of the self. The infant personality by itself is unable to make use of the sense-data, but has to evacuate these elements into the mother, relying on her to do whatever has to be done to convert them into a form suitable for employment as alpha-elements by the infant.

The limited consciousness defined by Freud, that I am using to define a rudimentary infant consciousness, is not associated with an unconscious. All impressions of the self are of equal value; all are conscious. The mother's capacity for reverie is the receptor organ for the infant's harvest of self-sensation gained by its conscious.

A rudimentary conscious could not perform the tasks that we ordinarily regard as the province of consciousness and it would be misleading to attempt to withdraw the term "conscious" from the sphere of ordinary usage where it is applied to mental functions of great importance in rational thinking. For the present I make the distinction only to show what happens if there is a breakdown of interplay through projective identification between the rudimentary consciousness and maternal reverie.

Normal development follows if the relationship between infant and breast permits the infant to project a feeling, say, that it is dying into the mother and to reintroject it after its sojourn in the breast has made it tolerable to the infant psyche. If the projection is not accepted by the mother the infant feels that its feeling that it is dying is stripped of such meaning as it has. It therefore reintrojects, not a fear of dying made tolerable, but a nameless dread.

The tasks that the breakdown in the mother's capacity for reverie have left unfinished are imposed on the rudimentary consciousness; they are all in different degrees related to the function of correlation.

The rudimentary consciousness cannot carry the burden placed on it. The establishment internally of a projective-identification-rejecting-object means that instead of an understanding object the infant has a wilfully misunderstanding object—with which it is identified. Further its psychic qualities are perceived by a precocious and fragile consciousness.

105. The apparatus available to the psyche may be regarded as fourfold:

1. Thinking, associated with modification and evasion.
2. Projective identification, associated with evasion by evacuation and not to be confused with normal projective identification (para 100 on "realistic" projective identification).
3. Omniscience (on the principle of tout savoir tout condamner).
4. Communication.

Examination of the apparatus I have listed under these four heads shows that it is designed to deal with thoughts, in the broad sense of the term, that is including all objects I have described as conceptions, thoughts, dream thoughts, alpha-elements and beta-elements, as if they were objects that had to be dealt with (*a*) because they in some form contained or expressed a problem, and (*b*) because they were themselves felt to be undesirable excrescences of the psyche and required attention, elimination by some means or other, for that reason.

106. As expressions of a problem it is evident they require an apparatus designed to play the same part in bridging the gap between cognizance and appreciation of lack and action designed to modify the lack, as is played by alpha-function in bridging the gap between sense-data and appreciation of sense-data. (In this context I include the perception of psychic qualities as requiring the same treatment as sense-data.) In other words just as sense-data have to be modified and worked on by alpha-function to make them available for dream thoughts etc., so the thoughts have to be worked on to make them available for translation into action.

Translation into action involves publication, communication and commonsense. So far I have avoided discussion of these aspects of thinking although they are implied in the discussion and one at least was openly adumbrated; I refer to correlation.

Publication in its origin may be regarded as little more than one function of thoughts, namely making sense-data available to consciousness. I wish to reserve the term for operations that are necessary to make private awareness, that is awareness that is private to the individual, public. The problems involved may be regarded as technical and emotional. The emotional problems are associated with the fact that the human individual is a political animal and cannot find fulfilment outside a group and cannot satisfy any emotional drive without expression of its social component. His impulses, and I mean all impulses and not merely his sexual ones, are at the same time narcissistic. The problem is the resolution of the conflict between narcissism and social-ism. The technical problem is that concerned with expression of thought or conception in language, or its counterpart in signs.

This brings me to communication. In its origin communication is effected by realistic projective identification. The primitive infant procedure undergoes various vicissitudes including as we have seen debasement through hypertrophy of omnipotent phantasy. It may develop, if the relationship with the breast is good, into a capacity for toleration by the self of its own psychic qualities and so pave the way for alpha-function and normal thought. But it does also develop as a part of the social capacity of the individual. This development, of great importance in group dynamics, has received virtually no attention; its absence would make even scientific communication impossible. Yet its presence may arouse feelings of persecution in the receptors of the communication. The need to diminish feelings of persecution contributes to the drive to abstraction in the formulation of scientific communications. The function of the elements of communication, words and signs, is to convey either by single substantives, or in verbal groupings, that certain phenomena are constantly conjoined in the pattern of their relatedness.

An important function of communication is to achieve correlation. While communication is still a private function, conceptions, thoughts and their verbalization are necessary to facilitate the conjunction of one set of sense-data with another. If the conjoined data harmonize a sense of truth is experienced and it is desirable that this sense should be given expression in a statement analogous to a truth-functional-statement. The failure to bring about this conjunction of sense-data, and therefore of a commonsense view induces a mental state of debility in the patient as if starvation of truth was somehow analogous to alimentary starvation. The truth of a statement does not imply that there is a realization approximating to the true statement.

We may now consider further the relationship of rudimentary consciousness to psychic quality. The emotions fulfil a similar function for the psyche to that of the senses in relation to objects in space and time. That is to say the counterpart of the commonsense view in private knowledge is the common emotional view; a sense of truth is experienced if the view of an object which is hated can be conjoined to a view of the same object when it is loved and the conjunction confirms that the object experienced by different emotions is the same object. A correlation is established.

107. A similar correlation, made possible by bringing conscious and unconscious to bear on the phenomena of the consulting room, gives to psycho-analytic objects a reality that is quite unmistakeable even though their very existence has been disputed.

10 Commentary[1]

THE distortions in "The Imaginary Twin" of the patient's past are designed to prevent him or anyone who knew him from thinking it referred to him. Such aims underestimate the power of rumour and suspicion.

If the distortions are judged effective, the narrative must be regarded as fiction. If the narrative were a work of art it might be reasonable to regard it as more nearly representative of truth than any literal transcription; but this psycho-analyst is not an artist. Expectations that the record represents what actually took place must be dismissed as vain.

The first paragraph is evocative; the reader is invited to appreciate the serious nature of the illness of the patient, the state of mind of one who has been advised to consider a severe brain operation, the pessimism and despair of one who has had so many years of unsuccessful treatment. The reader is prepared for the triumph of psycho-analysis in contrast with the patient's previous misfortunes under psycho-therapy.

Paragraphs **2** and **3** are factually inaccurate; the statements in the two paragraphs are representations of facts to which the realization did approximate closely. I thought this was true then; I think it is true now. What importance should be ascribed to these statements, one in the paper, made within months of the experience; the other in this book, made twenty years after?

It is usual to think that a report written within an hour or so of the events it is supposed to describe has a special "built-in" validity and superiority over the account written many months or even years later. I shall suppose simply that they are two different accounts of the same event without any implication that one is superior to the other. A technique is needed which will reveal the nature of the contrasting stories and of the contrasting elements in them. Historians are familiar with the uses of "contemporary" history

[1] Numbers in heavy type refer to numbered paragraphs in preceding pages.

and history written sufficiently long after the event for "passions to have cooled" and perspective to have matured. A psycho-analyst will require some more precise definition of the realities behind these distinguishing formulations.

The need for discretion means that certain facts are replaced by falsifications intended to make no material difference to the account of the emotional tensions which were part of the patient's environment. I have now no doubt that this idea is quite fallacious for the substitution is made in accordance with certain pre-conceptions derived from the experience of psycho-analysing the patient. The emotional background from which this account derives must include my ideas of what he told me, my interpretations, and my interpretations of the results of the encounter. When I wrote this I believed I was giving a factual account of the patient's behaviour together with a factual account of my interpretations—based partly on my beliefs about the meaning of psycho-analytical theory—followed by a factual account of the consequences of the interpretations. It seems to me now that it is more nearly accurate to regard this and all other articles written by me (for those are the articles of which I have most intimate knowledge) as consisting of statements of varying quality. For example, in paragraph 5 the statement is a verbal formulation of a visual image. Reading it now after seventeen years, I am able to receive a visual impression which up to a point reminds me of something that cannot be sensuously grasped—depression. The phrase "monosyllabic listlessness", coming in the context of the rest of the paragraph, makes me suppose now that the patient was depressed but it is not the same to say he was depressed as to describe him as being listless and monosyllabic. This is the crux of the situation; for the more unobstructed the relationship that the psycho-analyst has with his patient, the more subtle it is. It is an ineffable experience. The psycho-analyst's interpretation must be of a state of mind which it is the more difficult to describe in sensuous terms the more he aspires to be accurate.

In the psycho-analysis itself it is not so difficult to formulate an interpretation as it is here. To start with, the patient knows, because he is present, what the psycho-analyst is talking about. The same qualities inhere in the psycho-analyst's interpretation as in the association. Therefore the communication between the psycho-analyst and the patient has not the same difficulties as those existing in the written communication between psycho-analyst and reader.

The experience of the patient's communication and psycho-analyst's interpretation is ineffable and essential. The communication of this quality plays a vital part in any interpretation given to the psychotic patient. The patient's reaction to the interpretation often depends more on this quality of the interpretation than on its verbal meaning. Thanks to the nature of the psychotic transference, the fate of the verbal meaning hangs on the patient's reaction to the tone of the interpretation.

Now the sensuous image, C category in the grid, gives body to the description in paragraph 5. If I tried to formulate it in more precise terms as the scientist can with his mathematical formulae, the communication degenerates into verbal jugglery. Yet more precise formulation is required. if the reader is to have an accurate idea of the association that had to be interpreted. How is the communication between the psycho-analyst reading and the psycho-analyst writing to be made at least as effective as the communication between analyst and analysand? What has to be communicated is real enough; yet every psycho-analyst knows the frustration of trying to make clear, even to another psycho-analyst, an experience which sounds unconvincing as soon as it is formulated. We may have to reconcile ourselves to the idea that such communication is impossible at the present stage of psycho-analysis. Transformations of the psycho-analytical experience into formulations which effect communication between psycho-analyst and reader, remains an activity to be pursued. Some may wish to transform it into group terms, some into mathematical, scientific or artistic terms. Some may be satisfied to perfect interpretations in the context of the psycho-analytic session. No psycho-analyst will be content to leave things as they are.

A special instance of the problem of communication

between the psycho-analyst writing and the psycho-analyst reading, of which I have been reminded by preparing these papers for publication, arises when the writer and the reader is the same man. Here, one might suppose, are the perfect conditions for communication. Yet in the days when I used to write elaborate notes on my sessions with patients, I found that I was no more successful when the interval between writing and reading was relatively short than I do now when the interval is measured in years. At first I thought I could easily understand notes dashed off at speed, a squiggle here, an exclamation mark there, sometimes an interpolated conjecture or comment on my own feelings on what was happening. I will not say they were meaningless when I came to read them, but they did not convey the meaning I hoped to find. They resembled nothing so much as a sleepy note that I sometimes tried to make to pin down what I felt to be an important dream for study in the morning. The squiggles remained: the dream had gone. I found I could not make better interpretive use of them than of squiggles I made on the spot while fully awake. So it is with this paper here. I am not unappreciative of the account; I think if it were some other psycho-analyst's report I would think it quite good. But as it is, I do not recognize the patient or myself.

This sort of experience led me to try a number of experiments in note taking, including some, perhaps the most convincing, which were intentionally subjective reports on my feelings about the day's work. A card index served to find references to patients so that I might scrutinize the material quickly if I should wish to be reminded of his or her psycho-analytical history. This I thought helpful—once or twice. I have the same feeling now, for example, on reading paragraphs **8–11**, but I am not sure in what way this was a helpful experience then or is helpful now. Finally I abandoned note taking altogether but that was not till some years after the first paper was written. My reasons for doing so cannot be simply or comprehensively stated. One reason, relevant in this immediate context, was my growing awareness that the most evocative notes were those in which I came nearest to a representation of a sensory image; say an event visually recalled (for example see **5**). The evocation however was not of the past but of interpretations wise after the event. In short the value of the notes lay not in their supposed formulation of a record of the past but in their formulation of a sensory image evocative of the future. The notes did not make it possible to remain conscious of the past but to evoke expectations of the future. Using the grid I have tentatively constructed for this purpose, the statements made in my notes are better categorized as C4 than as C3.

In the grid these two categories appear close together. It is common in everyday life to hear of two people whose views are said to be "poles apart"; it is but one expression of mental "distance". The visual image of the grid suggests that these categories are neighbours and are we then to assume there is some corresponding "closeness" in the relationship of the *objects represented* by the grid? In the context of this discussion I am arguing that the actual value of the formulation categorized as C3 is in fact "far from" the real value represented by C4. Would the grid be more nearly representative of the realizations it is intended to categorize if these categories were differently spaced on the paper? The notes I am discussing can be said to belong to categories which are similar or close in that, if they purport to be records of the past, their object is to evoke memories presumed to be unconscious because they have been forgotten or suppressed or repressed: if they are to evoke ideas about the future they are to evoke prophecies or conjectures about what has not yet happened. The distance between the two, measured not in space but in time, might be infinitely small or infinitely large. Again, if my note tells me "what happened" in yesterday's session and makes me think of what is shortly going to happen in today's, can the "distance" between these two ideas be measured by the time that has elapsed between the two sessions? Perhaps it would be better not to think of it as distance, in space or time, between the ideas but rather in terms of difference relative to some scale with an entirely different genetic background from that of physical space or physical time. For further consideration—in what useful sense can it be said that the mind "travels" from earth to the nearest quasar with the "speed of thought"?

For the psycho-analysts these are not ideas but practical questions; consider the importance in a psycho-analysis of the psycho-analyst's or patient's ability to grasp an idea very "slowly" or very "fast". A patient may see the meaning of an interpretation so quickly that the psycho-analyst is surprised to find a moment later that the patient has apparently no understanding of what has been said to him. The speed of his thought makes him able to closure the statement being discussed before he has had time to understand it. The terms in which I am describing this are all modelled on sensuous experience of a sensible background. The model serves to illuminate many phenomena in psycho-analysis but the light that these models shed (this one included) is fitful and their inadequacy is easily apparent. The psycho-analyst needs models which are quickly constructed, widely applicable, robust. What we use now are short-winded. They serve well enough up to a point but that point is quickly reached and from it the psycho-analyst can see nothing but darkness beyond. That, in my opinion, is what is wrong with these papers on which I am commenting. I comment on them because their defect is not peculiar to these papers but to the method of which they are typical. The problem is to transform formulations such as "time", "distance", "space", so that the re-formulation is not so abstract that it becomes verbal jugglery and not so impacted with meaning that growth is obstructed.

The psycho-analyst's note on a session may be far from a record of what took place: yet near to anticipation of a future development. Scientific training seems to suppose that capacity for anticipation is a desirable attribute and worth developing. It appears important for the psycho-analyst to be able to predict his patient's attempt at suicide, or, conversely, his probable improvement. Let us examine this supposition more closely. If it is supposed that the psycho-analyst must anticipate his patient's suicide it means no more than that the psycho-analyst should be able to entertain as wide a spectrum of thought and feeling, pleasant or unpleasant, as is possible. The idea that his patient might commit suicide is only one particular instance of the painful thoughts which the psycho-analyst must be capable of sustaining; otherwise he will be deflected from doing the work he exists to do and which no one else can do, namely to analyse. If analysing the impulse to suicide cannot change the patient's impulse, prevention, say by hospitalization, will certainly not do so. Others have to fulfil different roles in such a contingency: they may believe that the psycho-analyst should fulfil these other tasks. Their beliefs may have disagreeable consequences for the psycho-analyst. The psycho-analyst only is in a position to know that his function is to psycho-analyse. He is under pressure, isolated and vulnerable, subjected to the temptation to abandon his role and assume one which, however unfitted he may be for it, conforms to the accepted conventions and preconceptions of the group. If he does so, the psycho-analysis is hopelessly compromised. The patient loses his psycho-analyst and gains a doubtfully valuable auxiliary.

The above arguments apply with equal cogency to the supposition that the patient might become a psycho-analyst, a supposition which the psycho-analyst should be able to entertain.[1] If he can entertain a spectrum of possibilities, from the suicide of his patient to his survival as a robust and stable personality, the psycho-analyst should be able to psycho-analyse each as it appears in the context of the psycho-analysis. The rock on which the analysis comes to shipwreck is the obtrusion of the memories and desires of the psycho-analyst; of this point I shall have occasion to speak later.[2]

At **12** commences a retrospective glance at the analysis. It is not my intention to question the accuracy of the description, but to use it to illustrate my present view. The account as it stands could be a description of either memory or evolution; they need to be distinguished.

[1] For important comments touching training analysis see D. Meltzer on The Relation of Anal Masturbation to Projective Identification. Int. J. Psycho-Anal. (1966) 47, 335.

[1] See pp. 143–5.

As the report of a memory it purports to describe my "memory" of what I now call an "evolution", namely, the coming together, by a sudden precipitating intuition, of a mass of apparently unrelated incoherent phenomena which are thereby given coherence and meaning not previously possessed. This I distinguish from the reports of the story told by the homosexual brother-in-law. That element, and others like it, I class as "memories" together with recollections somewhat deliberately and painstakingly recalled, as for example when a patient pieces together a dream he thinks he has had. In contrast is a dream which is recalled suddenly, as if in a single whole. Or perhaps similarly lost as a single whole. This experience resembles the phenomenon of transformation of the paranoid-schizoid position to the depressive position. I have in the past drawn attention to a striking description of the experience given by H. Poincaré in his Science and Method. The event described in **13** would do very well as an illustration of an "evolution". From the material the patient produces, there emerges, like the pattern from a kaleidoscope, a configuration which seems to belong not only to the situation unfolding, but to a number of others not previously seen to be connected and which it has not been designed to connect. I do not now regard the pattern of the "imaginary twin" as of any central importance, though I have found it illuminating for some aspects of the psycho-analysis of an only child. It is then very often a particular fact of the more general pattern of splitting. The patient of whom I wrote was *not* an only child, but circumstances led him to feel so. At the outset of his career, any psycho-analyst must find his own way and come upon well-known and well-established theories through experiences of his own realizations. It is clear that the realization which approximates to a theory he has learned will be unique and may therefore appear to be so different from the theoretical formulation that he cannot recognize the bearing of the one upon the other. By contrast he will force a theory to fit a realization because it is difficult for an inexperienced analyst to tolerate doubt and uncertainty which he imagines that a more experienced analyst—probably his own—would not have.

There can be no harm in errors of this kind: "original discoveries" of the already well-known and "confirmation" where none would be found if clinical flair were mature. It becomes fatal to good analysis if premature application of a theory becomes a habit which places a screen between the psycho-analyst and the exercise of his intuition on fresh and therefore unknown material.

The dream reported in **15** was I think as nearly in the patient's words as is possible. I assumed that it was correctly reported by the patient, correctly remembered by me, and correctly transcribed. There is no doubt that this convenient assumption is false. It remains none-the-less convenient and most psycho-analysts including myself will continue to use it —for most occasions. It is not always convenient and the modern trends in psycho-analytical practice will make these assumptions misleading unless they are used with circumspection. Failure to recognize the point at which an assumption, known to be false but convenient, becomes inconvenient as well as false leads to deflections of psycho-analytical practice into an impasse where pessimism reigns. I make this dream and the reports in **16–20** the subject of critical comment not because I have changed my views on the value of what I reported then, but because I require a jumping-off point for the exposition of something else now.

As I "remember" it the dream was reported by the patient in vivid terms. The report given in **15** recalled the episode, when I read it, in such "complete" fashion that I regard it as having "evolved" in the course of the actual reading. This is in contrast with my experience on re-reading **16**. I "remembered" that in my opinion my interpretation was a good one—"correct", as I would then have said, and I "remember" that the experience of dream and interpretation had the same convincing quality of reality at the time. The description in **16** cannot "evolve" anything now as the description in **15** can. I do not attribute this to the inferior quality of **16** but to a difference in kind in the nature of the two formulations. I find myself unable to be impressed either with the truth or falsity of the interpretation. With **15** I experience an "evolution" of emotional experience now;

with **16** I experience nothing but a sense of manipulation of theories.

As I participated in the reported experience I know there was no deliberate or conscious falsification. I also know that the formulation of **16** was as good as taking pains could make it. Even making allowance for personal defects in powers of description, the real problem arises in the lack of apparatus for recording the only part of a psycho-analytic session that is worthy of record. Occasionally, as in **15**, something can be recorded adequately enough to lead to an evolution when the reader is the psycho-analyst. Psychoanalytical literature has meaning for one or two readers of a particular article at most; it must be the dreariest and most unrewarding scientific literature for the others.

If this dreariness adequately represented the realization no great harm would follow: psycho-analysis would disappear, with other pseudo-sciences: to anyone who has experienced the reality of psycho-analysis the possibility of such an outcome of faulty communication is tragic. The formulations of **17** differ in kind from those of **15** or **16**. They are descriptions of events in terms which are themselves *theoretical* formulations of psycho-analytical intuitions. They are therefore removed from the world of emotional experience in a way in which the dream description of **15** is not, although, as we have already seen, the description in **15** is a description of a description of something alleged by the patient to have happened while he slept. As a practising psycho-analyst, I tolerate for the present the misgivings to which such an insecure foundation gives rise. I think the insecurity should be noticed but disregarded till it becomes relevant. The difference in kind between **15** and **16**, and then again **17** and **19–20**, is no longer tolerable because the nature of the work today does not permit of lack of discrimination between realizations which are so different from each other. The verbal formulation of the dream in **15** is, relatively tolerable; it can be regarded as category C3. The descriptions in **16–20** cannot be so regarded. They lack the immediacy which gives body to the description in **15**. Similarly, except to a few psycho-analysts, the formulations of **17** become theoretical statements of psycho-analytic intuitions which are vulnerable because they lack "body" on the one hand and scientific rigour on the other.

I tolerate the formulations of **17–18** because I do not see my way to producing anything better, but their value is debatable because what they communicate may not be worth communicating; conversely, what was, in the psycho-analytical experience, worth communicating may not in fact have been communicated.

The position with regard to **18–20** is more complex. I cannot now say to what extent the account given represents fairly what took place. I know that in intention it does, but psycho-analytical experience shows how misleading such an impression can be. Furthermore, I have since learned that no amount of psycho-analysis can insure the psycho-analyst against distortion of his material though his distortions may become less crude than they were before he had been psycho-analysed.

The account **18–20** is therefore subject to unconscious distortion of the kind present in psycho-analysis. Moreover the account is written with conscious aim to "illustrate" what I thought I had learned from the analytic experience. The need to "illustrate" the theme means that an attempt is made to represent the experience in terms of sensuous experience—C category terms. Description in such terms avoids the danger of manipulation of jargon but it introduces dangers which are as great though different. First the terms cannot represent the psycho-analytic experience which they purport to describe, but only a sensuous experience of physical fact supposedly analogous to the mental experience. **18–20** are a transformation (see W. R. Bion, Transformations) of an emotional experience into a verbal formulation of a sensuous experience (**19**). This is perhaps the most direct representation in the whole **18–20**.

In ordinary extra psycho-analytical experience, rigorous scrutiny would be irrelevant; possibly it would be irrelevant in most psycho-analytical experience. It is irrelevant to the man in this paper, but not in psycho-analyses of patients whose sense of reality is disturbed. It is essential to understand the nature of the psycho-analyst's formulations of his experience of reality to obtain a grasp of the nature of the patient's formulations of *his* experience of reality and thus compare the two.

The description in the last paragraph of **19** or the whole of **20** do not make clear how much the reader is to suppose that the account is a direct intuition of what was taking place and how much a report of selected facts. In psycho-analysis the psycho-analyst must discern the underlying pattern by a process of discrimination and selection. If the account given is a selection made to demonstrate the correctness of the original selection it is clearly worthless. Only if the original experience is a genuine evolution of a psycho-analytical realization, i.e. a precipitation of coherence by a "selected fact", does the writer's conscious discrimination and selection become legitimate as a method of representation.

In the passages discussed, there is a further complication because I had deliberately to falsify the facts to make identification of the patient impossible. This I achieved but at the cost of an account which I now consider worthless. It fails to represent the realization which I wanted to depict and it fails to explain the interpretations given.

This leads to the dilemma of psycho-analytical communication as it is at present. The report of a session (that is, the psycho-analytical realization) must be a literal and incomprehensible jumble or it must be an artistic representation. The former need not detain us: the latter, assuming the requisite degree of artistic capacity in the psycho-analyst, implies a transformation during which selection and ordering of the material takes place. The interpretation given the patient is a formulation intended to display an underlying pattern. It is therfore itself similar to the mathematical formula as described by Poincaré (*Science and Method*, Dover Books, p. 30). It is also similar to some aspects of a painting, sculpture or musical composition. At their best these formulations make us aware of a coherence and order where, without them, incoherence and disorder would reign.

In practice, the psycho-analyst does not possess the conditions, even if he had the attributes, for artistic creation—

unless we suppose that a capacity for conversational expression can be sublimed into a minor ephemeral art. He can however give an interpretation and the patient experiences the realization to which the interpretation purports to approximate. When it comes to psycho-analytic communication, the reader does not have the advantage of the patient. He depends on a verbal transformation of the psycho-analytical experience which has been formulated by the same person as the person who has made the interpretation in the terms he chooses to report.

There is nothing new in the criticism of lack of objectivity in psycho-analysis, and I am not proposing to waste time on it. I wish to consider a few of the defects which are loosely combined under this general head, in particular what the difference is supposed to be between the penultimate and ultimate paragraphs of **20**. To me the supposed report of what occurred is simply a not very good C3 formulation. That is to say, in order to convey to the reader an impression of the psycho-analytical experience (which cannot in fact be seen or smelled or heard, for one is not listening to what the *patient* thinks he is saying), a description is given in terms of what *can* be sensuously experienced. No wonder psycho-analytical interpretations give rise to scepticism.

Although no one doubts the reality of, say anxiety, it cannot be sensuously apprehended. In psycho-analytical practice, we are not concerned with crude examples even of anxiety; two psycho-analysts might disagree over a patient pouring out intense overt hostility to the analyst. By one he could be supposed to be driven by anxiety and by the other to be showing persecutory fear. The more experienced and sensitive the psycho-analyst is the more readily he experiences the non-sensuous phenomena unfolding before him. The psycho-analyst should therefore be able to communicate something that is at present ineffable. There should be a significant difference between the formulation of what is alleged to have happened and the formulation purporting to be an interpretation. What is the significant difference? What is the significant difference between what was expressed in the psycho-analytical session and the interpretation of it given by the psycho-analyst?

Psycho-analytical discussion often takes the form of comparing what the patient has said with the interpretations which were, or might have been, given. In addition to the objection that the psycho-analytical communication is two versions of the same observation, the psycho-analytical discussion demonstrates the futility of comparing association with interpretation. Associations are infinite in number and so are interpretations; it is therefore idle to discuss matching the one to the other. This is particularly the case since the report on the associations of the patient is a transformation and the transformation introduces a distortion which cannot be allowed for. The distortion due to the personality of the psycho-analyst does not remain constant between the association he reports and the interpretation he gives of his reported association. A student will sometimes report an interpretation which told the patient almost nothing more than the association has already said. In such a case, psycho-analysts consider the interpretation defective. There are occasions when the interpretation may be almost verbally identical with the association, yet, because the analyst is lending his authority to confirmation of the patient's statement, the interpretation produces significant change. It is therefore clear that nothing can be learned by a comparison of association and interpretation but may be learned by a comparison of the nature of the interpretation with the nature of the association.

In **22** part of a dream is reported. There are two words, "rage" and "terror", which, if it is assumed that they are correctly used, represent and communicate psychic reality. The context in which they are used is a verbal transformation of a visual image. Together with the terms "rage" and "terror" they evoke a powerful impression even now when I do not remember with any certainty the occasion reported. In this respect it is different from the reported interpretation which makes no impact; I do not doubt that it represents what I said at the time. Its lack of impact is not surprising because the interpretation is formulated in F6 terms. That is, the formulation is sophisticated and is intended to be the mental counterpart of action. It is intended as a psycho-analytical action. Like all F, G, H categories, it tends to come over as a meaningless manipulation of technical terms. This is precisely the danger to be anticipated with all sophisticated formulations. It is brought out by the report in **31**; the interpretations leave a sense of meaningless verbal manipulations. They lack permanence or durability; in this respect they differ from aesthetic statements.

At the time of the interpretation, this problem does not arise because psycho-analyst and analysand are able to compare the interpretation with the facts it purports to interpret. The reader cannot do this and no amount of description, however skilful, and no interpretation, however apposite, can make up for the reader's lack of the experience to which they relate.

If the psycho-analytical situation is accurately intuited—I prefer this term to "observed" or "heard" or "seen" as it does not carry the penumbra of sensuous association—the psycho-analyst finds that ordinary conversational English is surprisingly adequate for the formulation of his interpretation. Further, the emotional situation serves to make the interpretation comprehensible to the analysand although resistances require some modification of this statement as too optimistic.

As a result, interpretations which, when read, appear unlikely to effect a useful purpose, are in practice efficacious. Since it is important to understand the process of psycho-analytical growth, the failure to communicate the non-sensuous experience on which the interpretation is based is a major misfortune of psycho-analytic practice at its present stage of development. I suspect it also contributes to the somewhat futile controversy about psycho-analytical theories; the argument should illuminate *what* theory has been applied to *what* realization. In fact, it does not do so because no one has discovered a method by which this vital relationship between interpretation and the realization can be communicated. Even in **15** I was not able to make the relationship clear; still less in **23–24**.

26 reports considerable psycho-analytical mobility. The patient is able to move from one psychological state to another with some freedom. I do not now remember him to have felt "better" or to have used any terms which express some idea of "cure" or "disease". This was in conformity with his pessimistic and sceptical attitude but did not give any impression that depression was central. He seemed, even while he was speaking of referring his students to medical men, never to be consciously concerned with himself as a patient requiring cure. He must have been the first patient to make me wonder whether the idea of cure was not introducing an irrelevant criterion in psycho-analysis. This point will be considered again.[1] For the present I would draw attention to the contrast presented to psycho-analytic mobility by the moral rigidity noted at the opening of **27**. I shall have more to say of this later.

At the end of **29** and the beginning of **31**, I describe the problem produced by a growth of intuition. I did not then know how common this experience is. In the paper on the differentiation of the psychotic and non-psychotic personalties (p. 43) there is an illustration of an increase of intuition and the danger it represents for the individual's growth. The theme is developed more fully in Catastrophic Change[2] in which I explain that it is part of a widespread configuration. I shall leave that topic to discuss the use of terms such as "widespread", "superficial", used in the second paragraph of 30, and others drawn from realizations of physical space.

Freud's model for the mind, illustrated by diagram, is based on a realization of physical space; the linear representation helps to strengthen an impression which has not so far appeared to create any difficulties. It has facilitated understanding and discovery; but these models are inadequate for the investigation of patients whose orientation in space and time is faulty. If such faults are to be understood, the model used to investigate them must be one to which the realization approximates more closely than it does to the model used by the patient. If a patient behaves as if

[1] See p. 151.
[2] *Scientific Bulletin of the British Psycho-Analytical Society*, No. 5, 1966.

he were unaware of the passage of time and the analyst regards the passage of time and the failure to observe it as important, he needs to know how the difference of attitude has arisen. Of what is the analyst aware and how does he come to be aware of it? Does "time" "pass"? If it does not, then it is absurd to expect the patient to be aware of its "passage". Most people accept that there is a realization which is adequately represented by the formulation "time is passing", but a psychotic patient may not be aware of that realization and may not behave as if the formulation "time is passing" represents a realization of any significance. Would he accept the significance of the realization if it were represented by a formulation to which the realization approximated more closely? As it stands, the statement "time is passing" is made up of words derived from sensuous experience and is a verbal formulation in category C terms. Briefly, to grasp the nature of the patient's departure from "normal" it is necessary to have an idea of "normal" which is not itself a departure from normal. Psycho-analysts frequently speak of "early" and "late" phases of mental life. The discussion of episodes in the analysis as reactivations, or reminiscences, of breast experiences, implies an awareness of a dimension of time and suggests that some element which obtrudes has a history. Sometimes this may be expressed as having a "place" in time or a "place" in space—"superficial" or "deep". I have accepted this convention, but a problem arises when the psycho-analyst finds, as I have done, reason to question the usefulness of an interpretation based on acceptance of the convention. The complexity of the problem is increased when it becomes clear with certain patients that measurements of time and space are based on psychic reality and not physical space or time; both measurements are possible only to the patient capable of tolerating frustration because both are derived from measures of frustration. If the personality cannot tolerate frustration, he prevents the development of any apparatus which measures it. Thus, if he is so many years, or so many minutes from his objective, he annihilates space or time which measure his frustration. The development of more sophisticated usages of this capacity, such as measurement of time or space, is thus prejudiced. A state is produced in which the patient is unwilling to admit awareness of distance or time. Ordinarily this does not matter, but when I came to consider the nature of memory and desire, I realized that they were the "past" and "future" of the same impulse. Awareness of this led to awareness of a need to readjust ideas over an area which is too extensive for the mental comfort of the psycho-analyst. His experience is, in this respect, paralleled by the patient (see **32**).

Progress in psycho-analysis is inseparable from a need to tolerate the painful concomitants of mental growth; of which the immediate revelation of further problems requiring solution is not the least. The importance of this will become clearer with time; even psycho-analysts seem to be unaware of the expanding nature of their universe, partly because it is difficult to be aware of movement when the participant is closely engaged with detail, partly because the implications of psycho-analysis cannot be grasped at this early stage in its history. If my suspicion that this is so is found by experience to be correct, the difficulties of the patient, adumbrated in **32**, are significant for both analysand and analyst when growth is taking place. For the psycho-analyst, the problem presents itself for solution not only by the analysand but by the psycho-analyst as part of his own growth. He may develop contemporaneously with his patient, or independently, or not at all. In the latter case, the future of his practice or of himself is no part of psycho-analysis though it may be a part of the sociology of the practice of psycho-analysis. The psycho-analytical problem is illustrated by the difficulties to be faced on re-publication of the paper Notes on the Theory of Schizophrenia. As I judge now, the description given is a sound representation of the clinical realizations which it purports to describe. It represents fairly the experience from which they are derived; it points adequately to future recurrences. In terms of grid categories[1] (which I had not at that time elaborated), they are C3 elements intended to represent psycho-analytical realizations, C1 statements defining experiences of the psycho-analyst, and D4 formulations

[1] See end papers.

pointing to future contingencies. Yet continuing experience of psycho-analysis makes dissatisfaction with the paper inevitable. So it must be with any experience accompanied by growth; the valuable experience becomes outdated. The problem is to decide whether an experience which is illuminating to the psycho-analyst can be communicated to another psycho-analyst, and if so whether the communication is worth making or receiving; to this there can be no answer other than that obtained by making the attempt. Unfortunately, the time required for making the communication, for gaining experience which seems worth communication, and for receiving communications made by others, is so great that doubts of the value of the venture become intimidating. Nor can reliance be placed on hostile criticism as the ineffable nature of psycho-analysis makes it unlikely that so-called impartial criticism has any value beyond serving as an indication of the climate of opinion in which the psycho-analyst works. This may be summed up by saying that the psycho-analyst's work is lonely work, that the only companion he has is his patient and his patient is by definition unreliable.

Nevertheless the patient comes for psycho-analysis and no one can compel him to do this. There is therefore reason to suppose that even in the most hostile patient there is an impulse to co-operate. It is therefore of importance to know what significance is to be attached to this impulse. The nature of the problem is apparent when the patient is suicidal, or anxious to do as much injury as he can to the psycho-analyst, himself, or those who have his welfare at heart. The time, money and effort involved in psycho-analysis make it a useful weapon for the patient who has such an aim. If the analysand harbours such aims, it is evident that the analyst must be clear in his mind about *his* aims for being a psycho-analyst. An ambition to help the patient is inadequate, quickly grasped by him and swept into his system of attack. If the psycho-analyst has formulated any other aim he is no better off—the patient can detect and demolish it. In **35** I have used commonly accepted terms to formulate a diagnosis (F1 in grid categories). They have a backward-looking value and probably convey a meaning to the reader. The problem of schizophrenic thought and language includes the problem of the language that the analyst is to employ in discussing it. None of the terms used in **35** represents the state of mind of the destructive patient I want to portray. Yet the description is a representation to which some psycho-analytical experiences approximate. What then am I to think when I meet with these terms when used by others or, as in this instance, by myself? Looking back on it, it may be that all drug addicts, schizophrenics and obsessional patients should be suspect on the grounds that their destructive impulses approximate in varying degrees to the extreme I have described. A more useful supposition is that the psycho-analyst should regard the terms used in **35**, and others like them, as binding constant conjunctions, leaving the psycho-analysis to determine what the constantly conjoined elements are. In the instance postulated the significance for the psycho-analyst is not the nature of the constantly conjoined elements but their intensity. This is true, when envy, hate, sex, love are encountered. For the practising psycho-analyst the terms used in **34** are almost useless and I would now use them with circumspection. The patients in whom the difficulties described occur are important for the degree to which destructive ambitions are active. If the psycho-analyst could assess "degree" it would be as important as his ability to assess quality. The realizations of psycho-analysis are not however such that terms like quality and quantity can be used without considering their sensuous background. The measurement of frustration to which I refer in a forthcoming book may offer an approach to the solution of this problem. The models which a psycho-analyst is compelled at the present stage of psycho-analytical development to use, contribute to the difficulties of assessing quantity. A model is not the same size as the realization; it derives its value partly from that very fact. It is communicatively valuable to refer to a patient's greed for "the breast". But the patient's problem may arise not from his greed for "the breast" but from his greed for what he considers the world is able to yield him.

This alteration in scale, from "breast" to "world" can be an unobserved but outstanding feature of the communication as it is received by the patient, though of minor importance to the psycho-analyst who makes it. The reduction in scale may make the model illuminating in every respect except one—as a measure of quantity.

I do not propose any alteration of my formulations in **36** and **37**. They do not satisfy me now, but any changes now would be made without the support of current experience. They have most value if the reader will regard them as verbal formulations of C category elements. To me they are not reports on what took place. They are verbal representations of visual images which portray an emotional state of the writer at the time of writing. As stimulants to thought in the reader they could be useful to certain types of reader; therefore I re-publish them; I do not wish to minimize the importance of formulations which, in their time, served to represent experiences that contributed to the development of the patient and myself. If they had this merit once they may possess it still.

The last paragraph of **38** is a formulation which represents a realization that is recurrent. Together with **39** it contains elements of a configuration which is common in the mental sphere of groups and individuals. The recurrence of the configuration, though on each occasion associated with known psycho-analytical theories, leads one to feel there must be an underlying group to which all the configurations and associated theories belong. The instance cited is one example of a relationship, which I have discussed more fully since,[1] between container and contained denoted by the sign ♀ ♂. The sexual model implied serves to direct the observer's attention to a constantly recurring pattern; the diversity of the elements in its composition being indicated by being "in a group", "in a person", "in analysis", "acting out", "in a statement, word or expression", and so forth. It has been objected that, for example, "acting out" is merely a verbal peculiarity of an English translation. I am not how-

[1] See Catastrophic Change, p. 135 above.

ever referring to verbal expressions but to a *configuration* which may appear in a verbal formulation or in a realization, in a visual image or an emotional experience in one language but not in another; in one patient's conscious but not in another's; sometimes conscious, sometimes not; sometimes in thought, sometimes in action; the important element is that the configuration should be recognized whenever it appears. When emotional experiences betray the pattern, it may have a peculiar significance, but for the present I want to stress only the importance of recognizing the configuration wherever it appears. These words I write are supposed to "contain" a meaning. The verbal expression can be so formalized, so rigid, so filled with already existing ideas that the idea I want to express can have all the life squeezed out of it. On the other hand, the meaning I wish to express may have such force and vitality, relative to the verbal formulation in which I would strive to contain it, that it destroys the verbal container. The result then is not a compact communication but an incoherence. Or, to take another instance, a disrupted group or society, or a group leader manqué. Psycho-analysis itself provides an outstanding example of such a force, idea or individual in tension with its container, verbal formulation, or society.

The whole of **39** which I have suggested is most conveniently dealt with as a C category element brings into focus a problem which is of interest for the future of psycho-analysis. I have regarded C category elements as being the stuff from which the scientific use of models derives. One advantage of the model is that it does not commit the psycho-analyst to the formal rigidity of a theory, but presents him with a tool which he can discard when it has served its purpose. This may be soon, or only after a considerable lapse of time and after many experiences of the usefulness of the model. The use of models in the physical sciences is easily understood to be valuable because the material which has to be dealt with has a sensuous background or at least derives at a few removes from such a background. The sensuous component, which is by definition an aspect of C category elements to which those elements owe their expository value, is precisely the quality which lays the psycho-analytical model open to misunderstanding. The psycho-analytical model reproduces an aspect of the original experience, the realization about which the communication is made, in a new medium. It should display the invariants depicted in the new medium which are supposed to be discerned in the realization. But the psycho-analytical realization is not discerned by any of the physical senses known to the biologist. Freud in his seventh chapter of Interpretation of Dreams speaks of consciousness as the sense organ of psychic reality. It is not necessary to be a psycho-analyst to be persuaded of the realization approximating to the term "anxiety". Anxiety does not smell, it has no shape, colour, or other sensuous attribute. This is true of *every* psycho-analytic realization. The matters with which we deal are real beyond question, but have to be described in terms that from their nature introduce distortion.

The matters discussed in **39** require a model. There is no satisfactory psycho-analytical model; the nearest approach to the functions of a model is made by the patient when he speaks of the hole, the cavity left in the skin when a blackhead is removed. This model did not help him to solve his problem or he would not have come for psycho-analysis. The patient's problem is not the therapeutic measures required for a skin complaint, but the problem presented by his feeling that his "mental boundary" has lost an important part of itself through his destructive attack on it. He is now attacked by the "hole" which is the part of his mental skin which was residual after he had wrought his destruction. The statement I have just formulated is, as a model, inferior in sensuously phrased visual imagery to what the patient has said. What then is the matter with his model that he failed to come to a solution? What is the matter with mine that it is implausible and imprecise? In practise the defect of my model can be overcome because the matter to which reference is being made is at the time of discussion being experienced both by psycho-analyst and patient, and all that is necessary is that the words employed should be able to disclose an experience available to both *while* it is available to both. But when, as at this moment when I write and the reader reads, there is no emotional experience to which appeal can be made and the "disclosure" which I as writer wish to make is of an event that has not yet taken place—of an experience which in my opinion the psycho-analyst reading this will be likely to have, the failure of the communication is fundamental not incidental. The problem for which the psycho-analytical model is needed is similar to the problem which the mathematician solves when mathematics enables him to handle a problem in the absence of the objects. In the domain of the physical sciences, when the original problem does not permit the necessary experimentation and manipulation, a model can be built which will do away with the obstructive features while retaining the essentials of the problem unaltered—invariant. In the problem adumbrated in **39**, a model is required because the two "original realizations" do not exist, one because it took place in *circumstances* which no longer exist, and, in so far as it exists at all, it only "exists" in memory; the other because it has not happened yet and, in so far as it exists at all, it only "exists" in phantasy. Both "originals" are therefore not available for direct investigation. Is there some form of model which can do for the psycho-analyst what models will do for the physical scientist? If such a mechanism were available it could be used to take the place of the formulation in **39**. I think it would do away with misunderstandings which the present formulation invites. As it stands, it is a conglomerate of a number of different kinds of formulation, visual images, theories, statements which purport to be representations of factual events. Allowing for the fact that a more capable writer could correct some of these errors, I do not think that capacity to write well is the issue. There needs to be a recognized formulation which is understood by all psycho-analysts to display the invariants in an event which is unconscious because obscured by memory, *although* it has happened, and an event which is manifest because disclosed by desire though it has *not* happened. Memory and desire may be regarded as past and future "senses" (analogous to the mathematical concept of "sense" and applying indifferently to time or space) of the same "thing". Making use of sense in this way a formulation $\overleftarrow{\text{desire}}$ would have the same value as $\overrightarrow{\text{memory}}$, the former referring to an event that had happened and the latter referring to an event that had not happened and therefore not usually described as being "remembered". A patient who could be described in terms of conversational English as "remembering" something that had *not* happened would resemble a patient who was described as hallucinated. Conversely the patient who did *not* remember what *had* happened, through the operation of $\overleftarrow{\text{desire}}$, or *remembered* what had *not* happened, through the operation of the same agency, should likewise be recognized as belonging to the same underlying group of "hallucinosis".

The concept of "sense" which I have introduced has not been recognized in psycho-analytical practice and the psycho-analyst's armoury has been correspondingly deficient in observations of omnipotence and omniscience. It is quite common for psycho-analytic students to observe patients whose references to God betray the operation of "memories" of the father. The term "God" is seen to indicate the scale by which the magnitude, wisdom and strength of the father is to be measured. If the psycho-analyst preserved an open mind to the mental phenomena unfolding in the psycho-analytical experience he would be free to appreciate the significance of sense as I have described it above. As a consequence he would not be restricted to interpretations of God as displaying a distorted view of the father, but would be able to assess evidence, should it present itself, for supposing that the analysand was incapable of direct experience of God and that experience of God had not occurred, because it was made impossible by the existence of $\overleftarrow{\text{desires}}$ and $\overrightarrow{\text{memories}}$.

The experiences sketched out in **39** indicate the degree to which $\overrightarrow{\text{memory}}$ and $\overleftarrow{\text{desire}}$ obstruct the patient's relationship to an absent breast or penis on a level of mind, or at a time of life, when such an object would be so important as to evoke feelings analogous to what would in an adult be religious awe. This could be represented by desire. Taking the evidence in its other aspect, the sense memory, its significance would be its disclosure to the extent to which the patient's relationship with God was disturbed by sensuously desired models (or C category elements) which prevented an ineffable experience by their concreteness and therefore unsuitability to represent the realization. In religious terms, this experience would seem to be represented by statements that the erring race or individual allowed itself to be beguiled by graven images, idols, religious statuary, or, in psycho-analysis, the idealized analyst. Interpretations should be given, based on the recognition of desire, but not that they should be derived and given from recognition of the sense memory. The need for such appreciation and interpretation is far reaching. It would extend psycho-analytic theory to cover the views of mystics from the Bhagavad Gita to the present. The psycho-analyst accepts the reality of reverence and awe, the possibility of a disturbance in the individual which makes atonement and, therefore, an expression of reverence and awe impossible. The central postulate is that atonement with ultimate reality, or O, as I have called it to avoid involvement with an existing association, is essential to harmonious mental growth. It follows that interpretation involves elucidation of evidence touching atonement, and not evidence only of the continuing operation of immature relationship with a father. The introduction of "sense" or "direction" involves extensions of existing psycho-analytical theory. Disturbance in capacity for atonement is associated with megalomanic attitudes. The patient discussed in **39** had an attitude to the persecuting holes which ultimately showed features we find in a religious attitude to idols. The psycho-analyst must contrast the attitude disclosed in the pyscho-analytic experience with the attitude to his father, or his psycho-analyst, or the God that he is prepared to revere. In short the individual has, and retains, what religious people call a belief in God however much he denies it or claims to have become emancipated. The final relationship is permanent, though its formulation is subject to constant reformulation. Failure to recognize this vertex makes a balanced view of individual or group impossible and lies at the root of the supposition that there is a "negative therapeutic reaction". I shall discuss its bearing on the analysand's realization of insanity.

In **40** the analysand shows anxiety and hostility to what he calls schizophrenia and his capacity to be aware of it. The psychotic patient is subject to powerful emotions and is able to arouse them in others; so at least it appears until the situation is examined more closely. The psycho-analysis of such a patient soon reveals a complex "situation" rather than a complex patient. There is a field of emotional force in which the individuals seem to lose their boundaries as individuals and become "areas" around and through which emotions play at will. Psycho-analyst and patient cannot exempt themselves from the emotional field. The psycho-analyst must be capable of more detachment than others because he cannot be a psycho-analyst and dissociate himself from the state of mind he is supposed to analyse. The analysand cannot dissociate himself from the state of mind he needs to have analysed. That state of mind is easier to understand if it is regarded as the state of mind of a group rather than of an individual but transcending the boundaries we usually regard as proper to groups or individuals.

The psycho-analyst who undertakes a schizophrenic analysis undergoes an experience for which he must improvise and adapt the mental apparatus he requires. He has one great advantage in his relationship with his analysand which he lacks in his relationship with his colleagues and others outside the experience—the analysand has the experience available to his intuition if he will permit the psycho-analyst to draw his attention to it. Those excluded from the psycho-analysis cannot gain from the psycho-analyst's formulations because they are formulations dependent on the presence of the experiences being formulated. They are thus in the position analogous to one whose mathematical ability has not reached a point where it can deal with the problem of objects when the objects are not there. His position vis-a-vis the problem is similar to that of the man who has to experiment with the original object without the aid of an intervening model which he can manipulate. There is no brother with whom to work out problems of the relationship with a father. Or, as the religious man would say, there is nothing which can intercede for the individual with God. The lack of a counterpart to the model, the direct manipulation of the original, denies the psycho-analyst one of the the tools required for his job and contributes to the state of perpetual acting-out. This last is evidence that the psycho-analyst is not, and cannot behave as if he were, dealing with models (verbal or otherwise) of his problem but with the original itself. Psycho-analysis of the psychotic personality thus has a quality which makes it so different from the analysis of the non-psychotic personality. Conversely, the relationship with external reality undergoes a transformation parallel to the relationship with psychic reality which lacks an intervening (or "interceding") model. There is no "personality" intervening between the psycho-analyst and the "unconscious".

To sum up: the "originals" are beyond inquiry without the aid of a model. The fact that neither original is in existence makes it essential that a model should somehow make allowance for, and deal with, this fact as part of the problem to be solved, a problem of the problem so to speak, and as a feature that must itself be mirrored in the model.

Before leaving the discussion of "sense" or "direction", I must mention a mathematical feature of early stages in problem solving. The individual feels the problem is vast, or complicated, or otherwise out of reach. The model is an attempt to bring it into reach. When the individual is confronted with what, in comparison with himself, is an infinite number or quantity, he binds the "innumerable" host by the name "three" as soon as he has a feeling of "threeness". The "infinite number" has now been made finite. A feeling of "threeness" in himself has been "bound" and what was infinity is now three. Infinity (or "three") is the name for a psychological state and is extended to that which stimulates the psychological state. The same is true of "three". It becomes the name for that which *stimulates* a sense of "three-ness". "Three" and "infinity" are then instances of a peculiar form of model. They can be regarded as embodiments of a psychological state—like "father"; or like "father" they can be regarded as relating to or disclosing an inescapable state of mind peculiar to the human being. From one vertex, "three" binds a constant conjunction "won from the dark and formless infinite". It is a sign that precision has replaced imprecision. In what sense is "three" precise and "infinity" imprecise? Certainly not mathematically because the mathematician strives to achieve a notation which, however inexact its genetic background its role transplanted to a new domain is to convey the same meaning universally. In psycho-analysis precision is limited by the fact that communication is of that primitive kind which demands the presence of the object. Terms like "excessive", "hundreds of times", "guilt", "always", have a meaning provided that the object discussed is present. It is not a present in a discussion between analysts; when it is not present intercourse between psycho-analysts will tend to jargon, that is to an arbitrary manipulation of psycho-analytical terms. Even when that does not happen it presents an appearance of happening. The criticism of psycho-analysis that it is not mathematical and cannot therefore be scientific, when it is made, is based on a misapprehension of the nature of the problem and the nature of the kind of mathematics employed. The subject matter with which psycho-analysis deals cannot employ any form of communication which can cater for the requirements of a problem in the absence of the problem. It cannot even employ models which would provide an adequate substitute for the original of the problem. This has misled even friendly critics, because the language used by psycho-analysts often bears a close resemblance to ordinary conversation. Similarly statements made in ordinary conversation appear to say exactly the same thing as psycho-analysts—often better. I have heard a lay participant in a discussion on psycho-analysis in a BBC programme suggest that Freud said nothing we did not know already. When one considers that

Freud merely drew attention to the existence of sex, such a criticism seems to have a kind of lunatic truth. The reality of the psycho-analytical experience soon demonstrates the falsity of such a supposition. A statement made about a sexual experience, in the presence of the sexual experience as it shows itself in the transference, has a meaning which the same words in another and different context cannot have.

Before passing on to consider the differences between the psychotic and the non-psychotic personalities, I must make a brief reference to **41** in which results are discussed. I shall refer to the topic often because the progress of psycho-analysis has led to a departure from the state of affairs in which ideas of "treatment", "cure" and "results" had any meaning.

Psycho-analysis of the psychotic affords an opportunity for seeing what it means to work when insane. A distinction should be made in the use of the terms "psychotic" and "insane"; an analysand can be psychotic and insane and psychotic and sane. It is useful to consider one kind of psycho-analytic progress as being from insane psychosis to psychotic sanity. When I wrote this section I had not appreciated the extent to which ideas of cure, based on a background of sensuous experience and the pleasure principle, pervaded not only psycho-analysis but the whole domain of mental or spiritual life. Scrutiny of the synoptic gospels will demonstrate the extent to which the religious approach to the domains of mental life activates the apparatus of expectation of "cure" of "painful" emotions and experiences in a way which would be appropriate to physical pain associated with physical relief and physical therapeutic measures. It did not require that St. Luke should be a doctor—this is plain from St. Mark's gospel—or that Freud's background was a training in physical medicine, to trigger off expectations of cure which are allied to a background of physical pain. It could be summed up: "There is a pain. It should be removed. Someone must remove it forthwith. preferably by magic or omnipotence or omniscience, and at once; failing that by science". The conflict between the psychotic and non-psychotic personalities could be described as between a part of the personality which is religious and a part which is scientific. The contending views are alike in their bigotry. They are alike too in resembling contending personalities, success being marked by annihilation of the painful experience or awareness of it. Conversely, a sharpened awareness of painful emotional experiences would be a mark against the approach, scientific or religious, which was responsible. The psycho-analyst himself can act as if he embraced this view. It offers a simpler explanation and justification for the expense in time and money of psycho-analysis. Without it psycho-analysis becomes an activity which is hard to justify. Furthermore, it provides psycho-analyst and analysand with a "memory" which gives both the sense of security that comes from a feeling that they are not engaged on any activity new to the human group.

In a paper to the British Psycho-Analytical Society, of which an abridged version has been published in the Scientific Bulletin of that Society, I drew attention to the recurrence of a certain configuration which I described as a relationship between container and contained (♀ ♂). One manifestation of this relationship is in the stress between the "establishment" of a group and the "mystic" who is a member of the group. The stress is found also in the relationship between an idea and the statement (verbal, pictorial, or artistic) that intended to contain it. Psycho-analysis is itself such an idea. Any formulation of it, or person entertaining it, or group (such as a psycho-analytical society) harbouring it, will show evidence of that stress. The abandonment of a protective shell of familiar ideas will expose the person or group who abandons it to the disruptive (even if creative) force of the "contained" idea. Therefore "memory" is kept in constant repair as a defensive barrier. Prominent amongst these "memories" in a psycho-analytical Society is the idea of cure. It is a preconception in K; that is a preconception (Category D) which is *not* to mate with a conception, as part of K activity, but is to mate with a "memory" to become a saturated element (similar to a β-element) to prevent growth or catastrophic change. The psycho-analyst must not be surprised to find he is himself as unwilling as his analysand, or his group, to abandon the desire for cure or its idea. Nor can abandonment be achieved by an act of will. It is a short step from abandonment of "cure" to the discovery of the reality of psycho-analysis and the unfamiliarity of the world of psycho-analytical experience. The "desire" for cure is one example of precisely the desire that must, in common with all desires, not be entertained by a psycho-analyst. The reader will find evidence in these papers that though I had suspected I had not grasped the importance of this point.

The temptation to desire cure is intensified because anyone successfully undergoing psycho-analysis has an experience which resembles the popular idea of "cure"; it is supposed he is "cured" as a result of psycho-analytical "treatment". The idea of "results" should be similarly suspect because it derives from an attitude, common to physical scientists whose experience is related to sensuous impressions (though the intervention of apparatus sometimes conceals this fact). It would be ironical if an idea which the physicist is tending to discard should be taken up by psycho-analysts. We should be amongst the first to have realized the inadequacy of models in which results occupy a prominent place. In **II** I say that good work will be undone if the analyst reassures the patient: today I do not think it requires a psycho-analyst to reassure the analysand because the analysand can obtain reassurance through the apparent resemblance of psycho-analysis to the model of physical treatment and cure. Generations of experience of physical illness and treatment have established a model, a "memory", which acts automatically as a barrier against the intrusion of disturbing facts. Complaints against ineffectual psycho-analysis can be seen as the obverse of the comforting beliefs associated with models of treatment and cure.

Abandonment of memories and models derived from physical medicine involves experience of problems which the psycho-analyst may regard as outside his province or capacity; often they appear to delong to disciplines to which his training has not extended. The psycho-analyst's experience of philosophical issues is so real that he often has a clearer grasp of the necessity for a philosophical background than the professional philosopher. The academic philosophic background and the realistic foreground of psycho-analytical experience approach each other; but recognition of the one by the other does not occur as often or as fruitfully as one might expect.

At the beginning of the paper on the Development of Schizophrenic Thought (July 1955), I report that the attempt to give clinical illustration was unsuccessful and that I restrict myself to theoretical description. The idea that the problem of communication would thereby be simplified I regard as optimistic. The clinical illustrations I regard as C category elements. They resemble reports of past events, transformations of visual images, models, but they cannot be described as any of these things because they do not satisfy psycho-analytical requirements. No solution lies in applying "scientific" criteria as those are understood, but I cannot propose a better solution. Psycho-analysts who are not satisfied with the scientific quality of their work must look to themselves to produce better standards. The "theoretical description" to which I thought to restrict myself is only the substitution of a sophisticated formulation for a formulation employing terms with a sensuous background. An experience about which I had no doubts sounds unconvincing to anyone without practical experience of psycho-analysis. Conviction cannot be carried even from one psycho-analyst to another unless their methods of working are extremely close. So far this has meant that two psycho-analysts share the same theoretical armoury and this involves the danger that the psycho-analyst sees what he wants to see. If two analysts are successful in minimizing the operation of memory and desire, they minimize the danger of collusion and increase the chance of sharing the same experience—"seeing" the same mechanisms at work. The formulations used in this paper are verbal transformations of psycho-analytical intuitions.

Formulations of transference phenomena are unsatisfactory

though correct as far as they go. In **41** I would now employ a geometrical formulation (H category) as a means of transforming the psycho-analytic experience into C category terms, that is into a visual image. To communicate the experience in psycho-analysis, I use a sophisticated category (H) in a primitive way (C). In the paper I speak of the transference as if it were a linear link—a line without breadth, joining analyst and patient. But I see this now as changing constantly in the stress of the psycho-analysis so that the transference link, which at one moment is a line, at the next transforms itself into a plane. The psycho-analyst who is bound by the tenuous and tenacious line suddenly finds himself in contact with a "monomolecular" surface or plane. The patient has a precise contact with the psycho-analyst and the psycho-analyst finds his every fleeting mood reflected in the transference. Should he be irritated by the buzzing of a fly or a noise in the street or the impact of some grievous or dangerous communication about a patient or relative, the mood will be reflected. But so slight is the depth (or thickness of the planar transference) that there is no discrimination of quality of these moods. They have the same value; the buzzing fly or a serious and distracting piece of news, cast an equal reflection; both are observed by the patient, the one is of no greater and no less significance than the other. The transference change can be represented pictorially from "the line without breadth" to "the plane without depth".

Some of the difficulty experienced by analysts arises when the psycho-analyst allows the intuition achieved to languish and be replaced by what he has learned of his psycho-analyst's theories and experience. This impulse is easily stimulated and the habit once contracted is difficult to check; the effect on the psycho-analyst's intuition is first bad and then disastrous; if psycho-analysts permitted themselves the conditions necessary in order to "see" what is happening the realizations of psycho-analysis would assert themselves and the differences between psycho-analysts touching what they observe would assume more modest proportions. The problem of acknowledging indebtedness to earlier work is not difficult if it is excluded from the mind of the analyst when at work with an analysand.

The psychotic patient's hostility to mental apparatus, his own or another's, that puts him in touch with reality should be matched with his attitude to psychic reality. He appears to be peculiarly aware of, and persecuted by, psychic reality. I would not stress any particular aspect of it, such as the confusional states, painful though they certainly are, but to the whole of psychic pleasure or pain. The problem is associated with the dominance of the pleasure-pain principle, as would be expected, but it achieves its peculiar quality because the dominant pleasure-pain principle has to operate in the domain of endopsychic pleasure and pain. There is not therefore available the solution which is proper to problems of pleasure and pain which have their genesis in the world of external reality. It is as if the analysand felt he was required to deal with the kind of problem for which we now know psycho-analysis to be necessary at a time when at best he could only be expected to deal, in collaboration with a mother, with physical hunger. In other words, from the outset of life the patient feels his mental world requires special attention. This differs from having a *physical* endowment, say *physical* ill-health, which requires special attention.

With regard to the remaining sections of the paper, **44–50**, descriptions are unlikely to lead to error if they are regarded as C category formulations and used by the reader as "disclosure models".[1] They are to be read, forgotten, but permitted to reappear, as part of the evolution peculiar to a particular psycho-analytic emotional situation. The comments in the conclusion (**50**) are related to a vertex in which "cure" or "improvement" appears as significant; at the time I did not recognize vertices and had no reason for appreciating the inadequacy of the idea of "cure". My next paper shows clearly the extent to which I regarded this vertex as the only one. As it excludes many possibilities of which a psycho-analyst should be aware, I shall emphasize, by references to this paper, some of the disadvantages. In **51**,

[1] Ian T. Ramsey, Models and Mystery, OUP, 1964.

though I speak of developments "which are analytically significant", I really meant that they were therapeutically significant. I consider any idea that development is therapeutically significant as being of less importance than an idea that a development is psycho-analytically significant. The development might be considered both therapeutically and psycho-analytically significant, but the latter idea I regard as of a different and more important category than the former. In the same paragraph, I refer to improvements, but the "improvement" must be in someone's opinion and according to some established (but unmentioned) standard. That assessment is useful in so far as it purports to measure change, however vaguely; but the assessment itself has not significance (still less the only significance) for psycho-analysis, in the sense that "cure" and "improvement" have a significance in the domain of physical medicine. Assessments of moral or social worth are borrowed from religion or morals or politics without consideration of their applicability to psycho-analysis. This is the more surprising in that the analysand's criteria are proper matters for investigation. I do not question the "improvements"; I question the unquestioning acceptance of improvement as an aim or desire proper to a psycho-analyst. As I have said, there is no place for desire in psycho-analysis; there is no place for memory as it is based on and inseparable from desires related to past activities different from psycho-analysis. A desire to be a good psycho-analyst obstructs being a psycho-analyst.

I would today not go further than my last sentence: "the improvements I have seen deserve psycho-analytic investigation". More than that imposes a standard of progress which precludes observation of the different standards of progress, their provenance and part in psycho-analysis.

The limited acknowledgements to previous work may seem surprising. It is an aspect of psycho-analytic work of which I have become more, not less, persuaded. A psycho-analyst needs a capacity to see the implications of both what his patients and his psycho-analytic predecessors say and not the quantity of ways in which they say it. The implications of Freud's paper on Two Principles of Mental Functioning have been widely recognized by psycho-analysts. This does not mean that they have been recognized by any particular psycho-analyst. Memory as usual offers a quick substitute, in appearance at least, for permitting an evolution to commence in the reader's mind. What I have said about the psycho-analytical sessions I consider applies to the *experience* of reading psycho-analytic work. Freud's paper should be read—and "forgotten". Only in this way is it possible to produce the conditions in which, when it is next read, it can stimulate the evolution of further development. There is time to do this only with the best papers; but only the best papers have the power to stimulate a *defensive* reading (of what the paper is about) as a substitute for experiencing the paper itself—what I have elsewhere called Transformation under K as contrasted with Transformation under O.[1] The same comments hold for the papers of Melanie Klein that I have mentioned.

This view that psycho-analytical papers are to be treated as experiences which affect the development of the reader will not be subscribed to by all psycho-analysts. I do not contend that it is a matter of conscious choice determined by the reader's wishes, but that certain books, like certain works of art, rouse powerful feelings and stimulate growth willy-nilly. As everyone knows, this was so with Freud.

As I have expanded this theme in my communication on Catastrophic Change, I shall not pursue the matter further here. The works to which I have drawn attention here represent many hours of hard reading—which may not at first be apparent. I found them illuminating but they have not been adequate; though my paper is inadequate I am still at a loss to suggest improvements beyond what I have said above about the psychotic transference; I therefore leave it as I wrote it. The views put forward in **58** are more fully dealt with in my later paper on "Attacks on Linking".

In **63–68**, I have given a description intended to represent the actual experience of a session. I think that the experience was exceptional. The patient was co-operative within the

[1] W. R. Bion, Transformations.

limits set by his mental state and he regarded himself in some sort as "ill" and requiring "treatment". He also seemed to regard psycho-analysis as if it were treatment. I took this for granted as a reasonable view, but I think now that any view entertained by an analysand should be questioned. The psycho-analyst's tool is an attitude of philosophic doubt; to preserve such "doubt" is of first importance on which psycho-analysis can be built. A patient making attacks on linking will show his dislike for the analyst's ability to preserve an attitude of doubt and will make constant efforts to stimulate the analyst's desires and memory. The evidence of "improvement" which impressed and pleased me was no part of psycho-analytic work.

This theme is embarked on at the end of **68** and discussed in **69**. When a patient is so disturbed that he earns a psychiatric diagnosis it is not surprising that relatives, friends, the patient himself and the psycho-analyst tend to agree about "treatment" and "cure". But the most disturbed patient can show flashes of intuition which are reminders of his mental life often lost to sight. Conversely, persons showing powerful insights are often attacked as mad. In the paper on Catastrophic Change, I have drawn attention to one instance, well known in a Christian culture, and I pointed out a configuration in which this element is constantly repeated. It is necessary to be aware of "improvement" which may be denial of mystical qualities in the individual. The opposite error sees deep mental disturbance as evidence of genius. I leave that paper for further discussion but repeat reasons for mistrusting "cure" or "improvement", not because I doubt the existence of a realization which approximates to these terms, but because the tendency to equate psycho-analysis with "treatment" and "cure" with improvement is a warning that the psycho-analysis is becoming restricted; limitation is being placed on the analysand's growth in the interest of keeping the group undisturbed. With the conclusion **70**, I have no quarrel in so far as it can be regarded as a plea for more psycho-analysis; even so I regard it as redundant as psycho-analysis does not need anything that advertisement and political procedures can do for it. Conversely, those requiring the arts of the politician will not desire psycho-analysis.

When I wrote on hallucination, I thought "independent" support for the diagnosis of schizophrenia important. Now it is more significant that these patients are able to inspire similar reactions in members of groups to which they belong. The more intimate associates (relatives chiefly and the patients themselves) wanted to claim that there was something wrong, but that the patients could not really be "like that"; naturally what "that" was, differed in the opinion of the doctors from what the relatives thought it was. I did not appreciate it at the time, but by making a psycho-analytic approach I was presupposing yet another "that" that the patient was. I wanted support for the idea that I knew what the patient was; that the patient was what the medical profession said he was; that I agreed with the medical profession. I wanted to avoid the position in which it could be said that everyone knew what the patient was except myself and possibly, though not certainly, the patient. However that was soon the position in which I *did* find myself. As psycho-analyst I was committed to keeping an open mind, while feeling constant pressure, not least from myself, to take refuge in certainty. The patients showed themselves anxious to agree with an interpretation so as to build up a sense of security. Since I deprecate allowing rein to memory and desire, it is right to point out that exclusion of both exposes the psycho-analyst to the anxiety of being in a minority of one (possibly two when the patient throws in his lot with the analyst) by engaging on the psycho-analysis of such a patient.

Until co-operation evolves there is no question of "observing hallucinations". I do not believe this is possible if the psycho-analyst seeks the comfort of co-operation from anyone other than the patient him- (or her-) self. The psycho-analyst's position is not improved, vis-a-vis relatives, friends the medical profession and others able and willing to co-operate, by what seems to be an unco-operative and possibly arrogant attitude. Nevertheless, the psycho-analysis of a schizophrenic is done with the patient alone or not at all.

The "clinical" description, **72**, is open to the objections already raised against this class of report. The description is in terms appropriate to a sensuous experience. The experience had psychic reality which no one would dispute, but it was not represented by its sensuous reality. I cannot improve on the description I gave in that paper though it could not carry conviction to anyone who did not want to be convinced and might well put a strain on the credulity of someone who did. What then is to be done? I conclude that in addition to agreed procedures, analysis of the analyst and so on, there must be a conduct of the psycho-analyst's mental life which precludes his slipping into bad mental habits. It would help to avoid errors if, as a first step, psycho-analysts treated what are considered usually to be reports of psycho-analytic experiences as "models" similar to models used by physical scientists. Scientific method must be followed with caution to profit by Freud's demonstration of unconscious motives. Psycho-analytic observation of our own faults is liable to mask the weaknesses of existing scientific method even when recognized by scientists. The scientific method of psycho-analysis should be turned on its defects of communication. This is either meaningful, but inappropriate to a non-sensuous experience, or so "abstract" that it simulates but does not represent a non-sensuous experience. The choice appears as picturesque inaccuracy or jargon. It may appear pedantry to scrutinize the descriptions which we give of psycho-analytic experiences, but not when the discussion centres on hallucinations which are, as far as the patient is concerned, sensuous experiences. To the analyst they are not, for he does not hear nor see what the hallucinated patient hears or sees, but he must interpet the events which he witnesses. In **76** I mention my inability to report the "events" that led me to think the patient was hallucinated. I still find it hard to offer suggestions for determining the point at which awareness occurs. A patient may, for example, be making a series of hostile allegations. This can be a simple expression of hostility, but it may be part of a splitting attack on the analyst. On one occasion, the patient had no fear of hallucinations, with which he said later that he was quite familiar, but was using them as a weapon in his war with me. I do not consider here the *varieties* of experience with which the hallucinated patient confronts the psycho-analyst, but the psycho-analyst's experience of the patient's hallucination is usually a good example of what I mean by evolution. At one moment the facts appear to be a simple outpouring of hostility; suddenly they are transformed; the patient is experiencing hallucination. It is as if the psycho-analyst whom the patient was attacking had a "skin" which floated off him and now occupied some position between the psycho-analyst and the patient. (It is characteristic that in this description I have to resort to spatial descriptions which have more "body" than I like to give them and are known by me to be inaccurate formulations.) The more experience a psycho-analyst has of psychotic phenomena, the less room he has for doubt of their reality. They "evolve"; they are there and are replaced by a further "evolution". Fortunately for psycho-analysis, these events can be demonstrated between psycho-analyst and analysand, but unfortunately for the science they cannot be demonstrated *in the absence of the phenomena*. There is a curious parallel in the plight of the individual who cannot solve a problem of enumeration mathematically but has to resort to manipulation of the objects to be numbered.

In this paper I have described the evacuatory function of hallucination as if it were the only one. I would now expect hallucinations and the "use" to which they are being put to be constantly changing. The psycho-analyst needs to be in a position to "intuit" hallucinations and ultimately the laws governing them and their changes. A rigid system cannot represent a changing realization. Ability to banish memory and desire is one of the conditions necessary for observation of hallucination. The moment an evolution takes place and reproaches directed at the analyst have been "floated off" to an intermediate "skin" the analyst must be able to "intuit" and interpret it.

At **71**, I explain that existing descriptions of hallucinations are not good enough for practising psycho-analysts. The description I have just attempted may explain why I think psycho-analysts need to formulate their own descriptions. The transformation can be traced from hostile abuse of the psycho-analyst through its stages from fear of penetrating into him through violence of linear attack (and therefore confusion with him), to planar attack (the widespread, diffuse, unpenetrating associations) and thence to the "floating-off" of the "skin". I am not optimistic about making my meaning clear to the reader by such a description, but once he is in a position to *experience* the realization he will not have any doubts of its reality.

The psycho-analyst must not allow himself to be deflected from the vertex from which the emotional events, when they have evolved, become "intuitable". The study of hallucination is at its beginning, not its end. Time has confirmed the conjecture made at the end of **82**.

In **83** of the paper on arrogance, I rehearse the Oedipus myth by way of making clear a connection between curiosity, arrogance and stupidity; the connection cannot so easily be established in psycho-analytical practice. I found more difficulty when I was relying on memory to provide the links than I do today when I allow the analytic situation to evolve; then interpret the "evolution". It is essential for the psycho-analyst and his analysand that the operation of curiosity itself should be demonstrated and not its name. It has been objected for example that "acting out" is an English translation of a phrase used by Freud to mean something different from the meaning attributed in English to the term "acting out". The confusion arises because the discussion is thought to centre on the representation of a realization and not on the realization, or vice-versa, not about the *term* "acting out", but about the phenomena represented by that term. In the same way, I am not talking of occasions when patients use the word "curiosity", but of curiosity itself. The distinction must be, but is not always, borne in mind. If it were, the reproach of jargon would not so often be levelled at, or incurred by, psycho-analysts.

I state in **88** that the person on whose psycho-analysis this study is based did not at any time behave as a psychotic; this comment is valid if ordinary psychiatric usage is accepted.

Melanie Klein believed that psychotic mechanisms could be found in all analysands and should be uncovered if the psycho-analysis was to be satisfactory. With this I agree: there is no applicant for psycho-analysis who is without fear of the psychotic elements in himself and who does not believe he can achieve a satisfactory adjustment without having those elements psycho-analysed. One solution of this problem is particularly dangerous for those concerned with training. The individual seeks to deal with his fear by becoming a trainee, so that his acceptance can be taken as an authoritative declaration of immunity by those best qualified to know. He can proceed with the aid of his psycho-analyst to evade coming to grips with his fear and terminate by becoming a qualified pseudo-analyst. His qualification is an ability, thanks to projective identification (in which he does not believe), to preen himself on freedom from the psychosis for which he looks down upon his patients and colleagues. The more psychosis, or even hallucinations, are psycho-analytically studied the more inadequate established ideas appear; as I have dealt with this development in greater detail in Catastrophic Change I shall not discuss it here.

In **91**, the reference to the destruction of an important link is based on a number of observations, the cumulative effect of which led to the formulations in the paper on Attacks on Linking. The ideas set out in it illuminate a number of situations which I did not have in mind when I wrote the paper. As I became able to observe the evolution of the psycho-analytical situation I was led to the frustrating aspects of memory and desire. Analysands stimulate both elements in the psycho-analyst as a method of destroying his link with the analysand. It is as if the patient were himself a psycho-analyst who discovered these elements and set about deliberately to stimulate them to destroy the link between the psycho-analyst and himself. Experience of attempting to exclude the operation of memory and desire have persuaded me of the value of doing so. The difficulty of successful exclusion makes it hard to define memory and desire with rigour or to assess the nature of the sharpening of intuition associated with it. I regard the idea of causation, implicit throughout the paper, as erroneous; it will limit the perspicacity of the analyst if he allows this element in Attacks on Linking to obtrude. The "causal link" has apparent validity only with events associated closely in space and time. The fallacious nature of reasoning based on the idea of "causes" is clearly argued by Heisenberg, *Physics and Philosophy*, Allen & Unwin, 1958, p. 81, in terms which should evoke an understanding response in any psycho-analyst. Provided the psycho-analyst does not allow himself to be beguiled into searching for, and proposing, except in conversational terms, "causes", the paper may stimulate enquiries of his own. The discovery of a "cause" relates more to the peace of mind of the discoverer than to the object of his research.

This brings me to the problem of how the gap is to be bridged between reading the papers in this book and the psycho-analytical experience. My suggestion is that the papers should be read in the same conditions as those in which a psycho-analysis should be conducted—without memory or desire. And then forgotten. They can be re-read; but *not* remembered. Such advice could be given with greater assurance if the nature of the communications, their status as formulations, were more certain. I have attempted to make that so by proposing that so-called clinical reports (supposedly F3) were regarded as C3—verbal transformations of sensory impressions. At this early stage, there is no adequate categorization which is likely to be more useful than popular repute.

The proper state for intuiting psycho-analytical realizations, which I have suggested in this review, can be compared with the states supposed to provide conditions for hallucinations. The hallucinated individual is apparently having sensuous experiences without any background of sensuous reality. The psycho-analyst must be able to intuit psychic reality which has no known sensuous realization. The hallucinated individual transforms and interprets the background of reality, of which he is aware, in different terms from those employed by the psycho-analyst. I do not consider that the hallucinated patient is reporting a realization with a sensuous background; equally I do not consider an interpretation in psycho-analysis derives from facts accessible to sensuous apparatus. How then is one to explain the difference between an hallucination and an interpretation of an intuited psycho-analytical experience? The charge is sometimes loosely and lightly made that psycho-analysts psycho-analysing patients who are psychotic are themselves psychotic. I would seek a formulation to represent the difference between the intuition (in my sense of the term) of a realization, which has no sensible component, and a hallucination of a realization which is similarly devoid of a *sensible* realization. The psycho-analyst has at least the opportunity which would allow him to contribute an answer; many supposedly sane and responsible people transform thoughts into actions which it would be charitable to call insane and are often, charitably, so called.

As a stimulus to further thought, I would draw attention to a peculiarity, known to all but not sufficiently regarded. Ordinarily the sense organs have their own objects of sense. It is true that the eye, subjected to pressure, will apparently "see" light ("stars" according to pugilists). In the mental realm, the "sense organ of psychic reality", to borrow a phrase from Freud, has no such limitation. It can indifferently appreciate *all* the counterparts of *all* the senses. The mental counterparts of smell, sight, etc., can all, apparently be intuited by the same apparatus. The issue is of practical importance to the psycho-analyst whose analysand says, "I see what you mean" when he has a hallucination, say, of being sexually assaulted; what *he* means is that the *meaning* of what the psycho-analyst said appeared to him in a visual form and *not* that he understood an interpretation. This is the kind of problem to which the last paper, On Thinking, is an introduction.

The fact that thinking and talking play such an important part in psycho-analysis is so obvious that it is liable to escape attention. It does not, however, escape the attention of the patient who is concentrating his attacks on linking and in particular the link between himself and the analyst; such a patient makes destructive attacks on the capacity of both analyst and himself to talk or think. If these attacks are to be properly understood, the psycho-analyst needs to be aware of the nature of the targets being attacked. The paper is an attempt to elucidate this. With my present experience I would lay more stress, in **98**, on the importance of doubting that a thinker is necessary because thoughts exist. For a proper understanding of the situation when attacks on linking are being delivered it is useful to postulate thoughts that have no thinker. I cannot here discuss the problems, but need to formulate them for further investigation, thus: Thoughts exist without a thinker. The idea of infinitude is prior to any idea of the finite. The finite is "won from the dark and formless infinite". Restating this more concretely the human personality is aware of infinity, the "oceanic feeling". It becomes aware of limitation, presumably through physical and mental experience of itself and the sense of frustration. A number that is infinite, a sense of infinity, is replaced, say, by a sense of threeness. The sense that an infinite number of objects exists is replaced by a sense that only three objects exist; infinite space becomes finite space. The thoughts which have no thinker acquire or are acquired by a thinker.

In practice, I have found this formulation, or something like it, a helpful approximation to psycho-analytical realizations. The patient who suffers from what used to be known as disturbances of thought will provide instances showing that every interpretation the psycho-analyst gives is really a thought of his. He will betray his belief that papers or books written by others, including of course his psycho-analyst, were really filched from him. This belief extends to what in more usual patients appears as the Oedipal situation. In so far as he or she admits the facts of parental intercourse, or verbal intercourse between the psycho-analyst and himself, he is simply a lump of faeces, the product of a couple. In so far as he regards himself as his creator he has evolved out of the infinite. His human qualities (limitations) are due to the parents, by their intercourse, stealing him from himself (equated with God). The ramifications of this attitude, more clearly discerned if the psycho-analyst postulates "thoughts without a thinker", are so considerable that I require another book to attempt elucidation. Inadequate though this formulation is, I hope it will help the reader to find the continuation of the developments which I have tried to sketch out in these papers.

I would warn against the phrase "empirically verifiable data" which I employ in **100**. I do not mean that experience "verifies" or "validates" anything. This belief as I have come across it in the literature of the philosophy of science relates to an experience which enables the scientist to achieve a feeling of security to offset and neutralize the sense of insecurity following on the discovery that discovery has exposed further vistas of unsolved problems—"thoughts" in search of a thinker.

Index

Printed in Great Britain
by Amazon

27867255R00099